GREAT AMERICAN THINKERS

Thomas Jefferson

Architect of the Declaration of Independence

Andrew Coddington

Cavendish Square

New York

Published in 2017 by Cavendish Square Publishing, LLC
243 5th Avenue, Suite 136, New York, NY 10016

First Edition

Website: cavendishsq.com

This publication represents the opinions and views of the author based on his or her
personal experience, knowledge, and research. The information in this book serves as a general
guide only. The author and publisher have used their best efforts in preparing this book and
disclaim liability rising directly or indirectly from the use and application of this book.

CPSIA Compliance Information: CS16CSQ

All websites were available and accurate when this book was sent to press.

Library of Congress Cataloging-in-Publication Data

Names: Coddington, Andrew, author.
Title: Thomas Jefferson : architect of the Declaration of Independence / Andrew Coddington.
Description: New York : Cavendish Square Publishing, 2017. | Series: Great
American thinkers | Includes bibliographical references and index. |
Description based on print version record and CIP data provided by
publisher; resource not viewed. Identifiers: LCCN 2015051332 (print) | LCCN 2015051006 (ebook) |
ISBN 9781502619259 (ebook) | ISBN 9781502619242 (library bound)
Subjects: LCSH: Jefferson, Thomas, 1743-1826--Juvenile literature. |
United States. Declaration of Independence--Juvenile literature. |
Presidents--United States--Biography--Juvenile literature.
Classification: LCC E332.79 (print) | LCC E332.79 .C63 2017 (ebook) |
DDC 973.4/6092--dc23
LC record available at http://lccn.loc.gov/2015051332

Editorial Director: David McNamara
Editor: Elizabeth Schmermund
Copy Editor: Rebecca Rohan
Art Director: Jeffrey Talbot
Designer: Amy Greenan
Production Assistant: Karol Szymczuk
Photo Research: J8 Media

Printed in the United States of America

CONTENTS

"A Beacon on the Summit of a Mountain"

A mong the monuments in Washington, DC, there is one that towers above them all. It is not made of stone like the Lincoln Memorial, but is a single piece of parchment. It does not tower over the city like the Washington Monument, but people and nations around the world have looked to it as a source of liberty and justice. The Declaration of Independence is a monumental document that created a new nation and forever changed the course of history.

The Declaration is housed in the National Archives, displayed in the center of a grand rotunda between the **Constitution** and the **Bill of Rights**. It is watched over by armed guards, protected by one of the most advanced security systems in the world, and painstakingly preserved on a daily basis by a team of highly trained scientists who use technology originally developed for the Hubble Space Telescope to monitor for the smallest signs of

When Thomas Jefferson (*fourth from left*) presented the Declaration of Independence to the Second Continental Congress in the summer of 1776, he changed the course of history.

decay. This document was made from treated sheepskin, which has deteriorated over the centuries. It was written and signed in iron-based ink, which has faded to a rust-colored brown, in an ancient style of calligraphy known as copperplate, which is becoming increasingly difficult for modern readers to decipher. All of these factors conspire to make it nearly unreadable today. And yet its historical significance for creating a new nation unlike any other before or since—along with its message of equality, freedom, and self-determination—has endured for centuries.

Unlike most monuments of our political past, the Declaration of Independence cannot be separated from the men who created it. Although architect Henry Bacon designed the memorial for Abraham Lincoln, his name fades into the background in the interest of drawing attention to the man it celebrates. The Declaration, on the other hand, has been indelibly marked with the names of those who signed it in the summer of 1776, who pledged to one another and their country their "lives, [their] fortunes, and [their] sacred honor" in the interest of severing ties with Great Britain and securing liberty for the united **colonies**.

There was no doubt among the assembled representatives that they were in effect signing their own death warrants should the North American colonies lose the war with Great Britain. At one point during the signing, Benjamin Harrison, a portly delegate from Virginia, said to the slight Massachusetts delegate Elbridge Gerry, "I shall have a great advantage over you, Mr. Gerry, when we are all hung for what we are now doing. From the size and weight of my body I shall die in a few minutes, but from the lightness of your body you will dance in the air an hour or two before you are dead." Benjamin Franklin of Philadelphia, one of the Declaration's most famous signers, also understood the risk. He said, "We must, indeed, all hang together, or most assuredly we shall all hang separately."

Each of the signers of the Declaration of Independence shared a heavy burden. These fifty-six representatives of thirteen colonies spanning the eastern seaboard of the futre United States were prepared to make the ultimate sacrifice. But it came down to one man, a soft-spoken delegate from Virginia, to write the document itself: Thomas Jefferson.

Before the Bills of Attainder were issued in England condemning the signers for **treason**, before the solemn signing of the Declaration of Independence, before the boisterous arguing on the floor of the Second **Continental Congress** about the language of the Declaration and the efficacy of **revolution**, there was Jefferson. Over the course of about three weeks, Jefferson sat at his small desk in his room in Philadelphia, working away at the Declaration while his servant brought him cups of tea. When his deadline came, Jefferson delivered to the Congress a document that not only achieved the task of severing ties with Great Britain but also articulated the hopes and dreams of a downtrodden—and diverse—collection of colonies. It had been no easy task.

Jefferson's legacy is the Declaration of Independence, and the Declaration is the legacy of the United States itself. Jefferson's assertion of "self evident" truths regarding "unalienable rights … life, liberty, and the pursuit of happiness" has been the cornerstone of American society since it was adopted by the Continental Congress. Also ever since, July Fourth—the anniversary of its signing—has been celebrated as the country's birthday, and Jefferson's words have been its charter. Lacking the historical legacy of other long-established nations, the United States has had to rely on its ideals to bring its people together, ideals expressed by none other than Thomas Jefferson.

CHAPTER ONE

Jefferson's Early Life

Like many of the Founding Fathers, Thomas Jefferson's early life molded him into the influential man he would become. As he developed the sense of hope and human triumph that would serve as the foundational philosophy behind the Declaration of Independence and his policies as president, Jefferson also struggled with significant personal losses at every turn. Similarly, as he sought the prestige and recognition that came with success in the public arena, his quiet country estate constantly pulled at his heart. Jefferson's childhood and young adulthood were a prelude to the contradictions of his later life.

The Jeffersons were members of a long-established family in Virginia, having immigrated to the colony from England in 1612. The family quickly established itself in society soon

Thomas Jefferson was born in Shadwell, a
village on the frontier of colonial Virginia.

after arriving in the New World. In 1619, a Jefferson was listed as a delegate at a Jamestown, Virginia, assembly. Thomas Jefferson's great-grandfather was involved in land speculation near Yorktown, a profitable career that enabled him to amass an estate full of fine furniture, livestock, and even slaves, all situated on a large piece of land. Jefferson's grandfather, meanwhile, continued the trend of upward mobility and held a variety of prestigious titles, including militia captain, sheriff, and justice of the peace. It was into this heritage of wealth and power that Jefferson was born.

Thomas Jefferson was born on April 13, 1743, at Shadwell, a town in Albemarle County, Virginia. Shadwell was situated along the Rivanna River near the Blue Ridge Mountains, a mountain range that spans from southern Pennsylvania through central Georgia. The Jeffersons' home lay near the outskirts of the colony. To the west of Shadwell lay millions of acres of unknown North American wilderness. Jefferson's mother, Jane Randolph, was from one of the wealthiest aristocratic families in Virginia. His father, Peter Jefferson, was an accomplished planter, surveyor, and adventurer. Peter Jefferson was well liked around town and had a reputation for exceptional feats of strength. One of Thomas Jefferson's earliest memories of his father was watching him pull down a shed by himself after it had withstood the efforts of three slaves.

Thomas Jefferson reveled in the legacy and social standing of his family—and his father in particular—which tended toward the mythical. Peter Jefferson had made a name for himself as a surveyor, charting the backwoods of Virginia and beating back the forces of the wild through his own force of will. Though he lacked formal education, Peter Jefferson was a self-taught, self-made man. Thomas Jefferson wrote, "My father's education had been quite neglected; but being of a strong mind, sound judgment and eager after information, he read much and improved himself." Peter Jefferson, like his father before him, also held prestigious positions in the public eye, including colonel in the militia and member of the Virginia House of Burgesses.

Jefferson's father, Peter Jefferson, earned his living as a surveyor in the wilderness of Virginia, a job that required skill, strength, and determination.

Peter Jefferson had high expectations for his son. As a typical Virginia aristocrat at the time, he taught Thomas to pursue excellence and to be comfortable with power and responsibility. Peter Jefferson wanted his son to be like him: studious but not bookish, adventurous but not brutish.

When Thomas Jefferson was ten, his father sent him into the woods armed only with a rifle. The elder Jefferson told him he could only come home with evidence showing that he could fend for himself. Jefferson remarked that the outing did not go at well at first. He had no luck hunting, and the woods frightened him. However, his luck changed when he found a turkey that had been caught in a pen. He shot the turkey and brought it home. Jefferson's experience in the woods revealed his determined character and his ability to strike when the opportunity presented itself to him.

The interior of the Jefferson Building of the Library of Congress in Washington, DC. Before his death, Jefferson donated thousands of books from his personal library to seed the new national library.

A LOVE FOR LITERATURE

From a young age, Jefferson was determined to be a lifelong learner. He read the books his family had collected in their library voraciously. "When I was young," he wrote, "I was passionately fond of reading books of history, and travels." By the age of six, Jefferson had already learned Latin and Greek, and had started to learn the violin. Jefferson loved the instrument and music in general, as well as reading, which were pleasures he would enjoy for the rest of his life. In addition to Greek and Latin, he would add Italian, French, Spanish, and even Anglo-Saxon (also known as Old English, the language of *Beowulf*) to his repertoire of languages. He kept notebooks on a variety of subjects, from literature and philosophy to gardening and meteorology. In fact, Jefferson's profound intelligence led President John F. Kennedy to remark at a state dinner honoring Nobel Prize recipients, "I think this is the most extraordinary collection of talent, of human knowledge, that has ever been gathered together at the White House, with the possible exception of when Thomas Jefferson dined alone."

The Emotional Resilience of Jane Randolph

In 1752, when he was just fourteen, Thomas Jefferson's father died at the age of forty-nine. Thomas, as eldest son, became the man of the house. Jefferson had, up until this point, spent many nights with his father in the family's study, discussing books and listening to the elder Jefferson's stories about adventures in the wildernesses of the New World. Although his father had died, Jefferson continued his habit of reading and thinking deeply in the study, as if his father's spirit was still present with him in this room.

Jefferson's mother, Jane Randolph Jefferson, was left in charge of the household, which included eight children, sixty-six slaves, and 2,750 acres (1,112 hectares) of land. Managing a bustling plantation was no small feat for anyone, let alone someone who was grieving following the loss of her spouse. In addition, with medicine and childbirth being what it was in the mid-eighteenth century, Jane Randolph had to deal with the losses of several of her children at a young age. Of those that survived, it seems that one of them, Elizabeth, was born with a disability.

Perhaps the greatest ordeal to strike the Jefferson family occurred early in the year of 1770. On Thursday, February 1, while Jefferson and his mother were visiting a neighbor, they received word that Shadwell had burned down. The Jeffersons returned to find nearly everything they owned destroyed. When Jefferson asked the slaves at the plantation about the fate of his library, they replied, "No master, all burnt, but we save your fiddle." The loss of Jefferson's books was a hard blow, as he wrote to his friend, John Page. Although he calculated the economic loss to be about two hundred pounds, he wrote, "Would to God it had been the money … [that would have] never cost me a sigh!" Although the Jeffersons had lost nearly everything, their matriarch, Jane, endeavored to rebuild the plantation where it used to stand rather than to move, choosing to shape her own reality in the face of such tragedy.

Jane Jefferson would manage the loss of her husband, the management of the estate, and many more tragedies with a sort of **stoic** grace. Regarding his mother, Jefferson wrote, "The most fortunate of us in all our journey through life frequently meet with calamities and misfortunes which greatly afflict us … to fortify our minds against the attacks of these calamities and misfortunes should be one of the principal studies and endeavors of ours lives." If Jefferson learned from his father the dignity and manners of a public personage, from his mother he learned the art of emotional control through her strength during this onslaught of personal tragedy.

Jefferson's Education

When he was nine, Jefferson began his formal education. Later in life, he was not shy about offering his opinions of his teachers, He considered one of them, his classical languages and French tutor, Reverend William Douglas, to be mediocre—not surprising considering he had already been studying the classics for years before he met Douglas for instruction.

During this time, Jefferson became close friends with a schoolmate named Dabney Carr. Jefferson and Carr were the same age and shared a passion for literature and the outdoors. When on break from their studies, the two of them spent their time at the Jefferson family's estate, hiking with their books to the summit of what Carr called "Tom's Mountain." While there, sitting under a particular oak tree, the two talked and brainstormed together.

Jefferson and Carr were fierce friends. Years later, Jefferson would celebrate his friend with the highest of praise. "His character was of a high order," Jefferson wrote. "A spotless integrity, sound judgment, handsome imagination, enriched by education and reading, quick and clear in his conceptions, of correct and ready elocution, impressing every hearer with the sincerity of the heart from which it flowed." Their friendship was both lighthearted in its humor and intense in its seriousness. At some point during their time up on Tom's Mountain, they made an agreement: Whoever died first would be buried by the other under their oak tree. When Carr died in 1773 at the age of

Jefferson designed his home, Monticello, himself, drawing inspiration from ancient Roman and neoclassical structures. Today, thousands of visitors tour it every year.

thirty, Jefferson made good on his promise, interring his friend on the new estate he had built on his father's land, which Jefferson now called **Monticello**.

Over the winter of 1759–1760, Jefferson traveled to Chatsworth, an estate located near the James River and owned by Jane Randolph's cousin, Peter Randolph. During the holidays, Randolph encouraged Jefferson, now almost seventeen, to enroll at the College of William and Mary, located in Williamsburg, the capital of colonial Virginia.

MONTICELLO: THOMAS JEFFERSON'S LITTLE MOUNTAIN

When Jefferson inherited his father's 5,000 acre (2,023 ha) plantation at the age of twnty-six, he chose to build a new home for himself, where he and his friend Dabney Carr spent their days together. Jefferson designed Monticello himself, despite having no formal training in architecture. Rather, he learned how to design and build a house as he had always learned: by himself. He read deeply on architecture, studying both the structures erected by the ancient Romans as well as the achievements of Italian architects during the Renaissance, including the villas of Andrea Palladio. Given these influences, Monticello is a perfect example of **neoclassical** design. Jefferson's architectural accomplishments did not end at Monticello, however; Jefferson also designed the Virginia state capitol and the central buildings of the University of Virginia, both of which are still in use today.

Monticello was a continuing project throughout Jefferson's life. Jefferson began building Monticello in 1772, starting out in a small one-room cottage. He continued for ten years until the death of his wife in 1782 stopped progress. Jefferson resumed construction again in 1796 after returning from France, bringing with him new inspiration from French architects. Jefferson also had to continue expanding his home in order to accommodate his collections of furniture, books, and gadgets, which included a rotating bookshelf, a copying machine, and toenail clippers. Jefferson largely completed Monticello when he retired from public office in 1809, though he continued to putter around his home for the rest of his life.

Jefferson so loved his estate that he wrote, "I am as happy no where else and in no other society, and all my wishes end, where I hope my days will end, at Monticello." Jefferson was granted his wish; he died in his room at Monticello in 1826 and was buried alongside his friends and family in the Monticello cemetery. The Thomas Jefferson Memorial Foundation has maintained Monticello since 1923. In 1987, Monticello was named a UNESCO World Heritage Site. According to the Charlottesville Albemarle Convention and Visitors Bureau, Monticello hosts 450,000 visitors each year.

The Sir Christopher Wren building of the College of William and Mary, Jefferson's alma mater, is the oldest college building in the United States.

Chartered in 1693, William and Mary is the second-oldest institute for higher learning in the United States after Harvard and continues to educate students today. In Jefferson's time, the school had a long list of accomplished alumni, including future presidents George Washington and James Monroe, future Supreme Court chief justice John Marshall, and over a dozen Virginia governors. Jefferson applied and was accepted. Soon after, he traveled to the capital city.

The Big City, the Wider World

Jefferson was enrolled full-time at William and Mary from the ages of seventeen to nineteen. Afterward, he studied law at the college for five more years, during which time he moved from Williamsburg to other locations in Virginia.

At the center of William and Mary was the Wren Building, designed by the renowned English architect Sir Christopher Wren. (The Wren building is still in use today, making it the oldest college building in the United States.) Situated on Duke of Gloucester Street, the Wren Building was on the same street as both the royal governor's palace and the Virginia capitol building, which featured both the House of Burgesses (colonial Virginia's **legislature**) and the General Court (the colony's court of law). The College's proximity to the center of colonial government in Virginia fired Jefferson's passion for public life.

As an intellectual and a bon vivant, Jefferson thrived in Williamsburg. Its bookstores featured the latest titles, and the city's successful men earned his admiration. However, the city offered more than just intellectual excitement. Attractive young women caught his eye, and social events such as horse racing, fox hunts, and dances drew his attention away from his education.

At first, Jefferson was caught up in all the distractions Williamsburg had to offer. He gambled, he hunted, he raced, he danced, and he dated the many beautiful young ladies that lived in the capital. Jefferson wrote:

> I was often thrown into the society of horse racers, card players, fox hunters, scientific and professional men, and of dignified men, and many a time have I asked myself, in the enthusiastic moment of the death of a fox, the victory of a favorite horse, the issue of a question eloquently argued at the bar, or in the great council of the nation, well, which of these kinds of reputation should I prefer? That of a horse jockey? a fox hunter? an orator? or the honest advocate of my country's rights?

When his first year ended and Jefferson returned home for the summer, he realized that he had largely wasted his time in

Williamsburg. Like many college students, Jefferson had been distracted by the relative freedom he had found at school. During that summer, Jefferson reflected on the incredible opportunity presented to him to devote himself to study with few other real-world obligations, and he resolved to take his schoolwork more seriously. "Of all cankers of human happiness," Jefferson later wrote his daughter about his time at school, "none corrodes it with so silent, yet so baneful, a tooth, as indolence."

His friend Dabney Carr joined Jefferson at William and Mary the following year. Partly inspired by his friend's presence and with his newfound dedication in mind, Jefferson buckled down to the rigorous habit of scholarship. It is said that Jefferson began each day at dawn, studying all the way through until two a.m. By this time, Jefferson had begun to think about a career in law. As such, he divided his time among four subjects: he studied law, on which he spent the most time, in the mornings, and the rest of his time he spent on history, philosophy, and poetry.

Jefferson, as his father had wished when he was a child, did not simply live in his mind, however. He also kept a strict physical exercise routine, upholding the ancient Greek maxim "a sound mind in a sound body." Each night in the early evening, Jefferson ran to a stone located a mile outside of Williamsburg. During his time at home, Jefferson rowed a boat along the Rivanna and hiked in the mountains. He kept this routine through all types of weather, even during periods of heavy rain and cold; in fact, Jefferson considered exercise in the elements to be fortifying. Jefferson thought that exercising in the pouring rain was as dangerous to a person's health as taking a cold bath. (He was on to something, as modern science has shown that taking a cold bath or shower helps improve circulation.) "Brute animals are the most healthy, and they are exposed to all weather, and of men, those are healthiest who are the most exposed," Jefferson said. Like his intrepid father before him, Jefferson was undeterred by the weather and dared to brave the elements.

Young Love

While in Williamsburg, Jefferson would discover another of his great passions in life: women. Among the young women of the colonial capital, one in particular caught his eye. Her name was Rebecca Lewis Burwell, sister to one of Jefferson's classmates. Like many adolescent young men, Jefferson pined desperately after Burwell, writing lengthy letters to his friends about his abject depression at being unable to be with her.

On the evening of October 6, 1763, Jefferson would experience utter defeat in love. Williamsburg's Raleigh Tavern was hosting a dance, and both Jefferson and Burwell were in attendance. Jefferson was determined to express his affection for Burwell then and there. Jefferson wrote that he had gone over the exchange in his mind, much like a modern young man psyching himself up in front of his bathroom mirror. "I was prepared to say a great deal: I had dressed up in my own mind such thoughts as occurred to me, in as moving language as I knew how, and expected to have performed in a tolerably creditable manner," he said. While he was dancing with Burwell, Jefferson decided to express his affection. When he opened his mouth to speak, however, he could only blurt out a few of his disjointed thoughts in between long, awkward pauses—a far cry from the eloquent outpouring of poetic love he had planned to deliver. Rebecca turned him down.

Jefferson took the rejection hard. His disappointment over Burwell was one of the first in a repeated pattern of aspiration, rejection, and dejection. Perhaps as a result of this stress, Jefferson experienced the first of chronic **migraines** that would plague him throughout his life. These "periodical head aches," as Jefferson called them, sometimes lasted days at a time and frequently prevented Jefferson from accomplishing anything. He complained of being forced to stop reading, and sometimes even thinking at all, as a result of these migraines.

Jefferson chased a handful of other women both during his time in Williamsburg as well as after he left but experienced similar luck. Ultimately, Jefferson married a widow, Martha Wayles Skelton, known to friends as Patty, in January 1772. Patty was the daughter of John Wayles, a self-made man born in England. Wayles had made his living as a slave trader and planter, among other things. No portraits of Patty Jefferson are known to exist, but she was said to be strikingly beautiful, with charming brown eyes and lovely reddish-brown hair.

More important than good looks, though, Patty was an intellectual companion to Jefferson. She was both well-read and strong-willed, and Jefferson could confide his internal struggles in her and find reassurance. Jefferson loved her passionately. During their marriage, which lasted ten years, his wife became pregnant six times. However, only two daughters—Martha and Mary Jefferson—survived to adulthood.

Budding Philosophy

Among Jefferson's professors, few were as favored by the future founding father as Dr. William Small, who hailed from Scotland. "It was my great good fortune," Jefferson wrote, "and what probably fixed the destinies of my life" that he got to study with him. Jefferson studied mathematics, which he called a "useful branch of science," under Small. Small also taught ethics, rhetoric, literature, and natural sciences. However, it was Small's worldview based on **Enlightenment** ideals that truly captivated Jefferson.

The Enlightenment was a defining period in western (especially western European) philosophy that began around the mid-seventeenth century. During this time, people started to think about the nature of knowledge and how humans come to truly know what they know, giving rise to the principle known as **humanism**. The Enlightenment concluded that people discover knowledge through analytical study. For example, a person might come to understand the workings of political philosophy by thinking deeply about the topic and observing how people behave in political systems. While this might seem obvious to modern students, up until the Enlightenment, people in the west put their trust in centuries-old traditions, many of which verged on the superstitious, that held no basis in the real world. During this time, most people believed in the "divine right of kings," which maintained that the monarchies of Europe justly derived their powers from a mandate given to them by God. There was no question as to whether this was true or if there could be a more just distribution of power—it was just so. To suggest that human beings could study things such as the natural world, society, and the human mind through observation and careful reasoning set the world on its head. As the famous German Enlightenment philosopher Immanuel Kant wrote, "Dare to know. Have the courage to use your own understanding."

Small, and Jefferson after him, came to share the **liberal** ideals of reason and individual liberty that grew out of the Enlightenment. Small introduced Jefferson to the writings of English and Scottish Enlightenment thinkers: the scientists Francis Bacon and Isaac Newton, the political philosopher John Locke, and the economist Adam Smith. Locke's theories about just government and Smith's writings on market economies in particular would have a large impact on Jefferson's own philosophy and, as a result, the foundation of the future United States itself. Small left such an imprint on Jefferson's life that Jefferson considered his professor to be a father to him.

Small also introduced his protégé to other great men in Williamsburg, such as the royal governor, Francis Fauquier, and lawyer George Wythe. Fauquier liked to invite his friends over to the Governor's Palace for eating, drinking, card playing, talking, and dancing. When Fauquier, who was a great lover of music, heard of

Jefferson's talent with the violin, he invited Jefferson to join the three of them on evenings in the mansion.

Jefferson spent a large part of these evenings talking with George Wythe, one of Virginia's most celebrated attorneys. (Today, Wythe's name graces the building that houses the William and Mary law school.) During their conversations, Wythe introduced Jefferson to the practice of law, a field that would draw Jefferson's attention from that point up to the American Revolution, when his attention would be drawn to matters of state.

Also among Jefferson's familiars in Williamsburg was his cousin, Peyton Randolph. Twenty-two years Jefferson's senior, Randolph held many respectable positions in pre-revolution Virginia: attorney general, Speaker of the House of Burgesses, and in due time, president of the first Continental Congress. Together with Dr. Small and George Wythe, Peyton Randolph was the third man with whom Jefferson formed a sort of cabinet of advisors. The desire to achieve their commendation guided Jefferson in many scenarios. After Jefferson left Williamsburg, he would use their example as a personal guide, even during his presidency. "Under temptations and difficulties," Jefferson wrote, "I would ask myself—what would Dr. Small, Mr. Wythe, Peyton Randolph do in this situation?"

All of these experiences—from his habit of industrious study, his enlightening conversations with Dr. Small, his familiarity with Williamsburg's movers and shakers, and his participation in the city's vibrant social life—combined to make Jefferson's time in Virginia's capital the most formative on his path to the public area. Jefferson learned to be social and make connections, skills which grew stronger as he continued to read deeply. At Williamsburg he became a man about town and a man of the town; soon, he would be a man of the colony itself and of the nation as a whole.

CHAPTER TWO

The Brewing Revolution

Just as Thomas Jefferson was coming into his destiny as a public visionary, the North American colonies were in a state of tension that would soon need a leader to step forward and guide them into a new era. During the decade after Jefferson had started at William and Mary, the relationship between Great Britain and the colonies grew increasingly strained. Britain began taxing the American colonies, who were not represented in the British Parliament. Without a say in the taxes they would be required to pay, the colonists grew angry. This tension culminated in an American war for independence.

Taxation Begins

The first of Britain's taxes was known as the Sugar Act of 1764, which modified an earlier tax placed on sugar and molasses that

Just as Jefferson was coming into his own as a lawyer and politician, many in the American colonies were starting to consider separating from Great Britain. They would soon need a visionary statesman like Jefferson to lead them.

THE LONG STRUGGLE
FOR LIBERTY

The roots of rebellion in America can be traced back to the French and Indian War, the name given to the battles fought in North America during the Seven Years' War (or, to the English, the Great War for the Empire). From 1756 through 1763, Britain fought with France over control in the New World and Europe. Although fought on three continents, including Europe, Asia, and North America, the bulk of the fighting took place between the British and French colonies in America. The conflict with France and Britain had been growing for years and contributed in large part to the explosive growth of the colonies in the first half of the eighteenth century. In order to rival the French colonies and provide enough raw materials needed to wage war, the population in the colonies quintupled in size, from 250,000 in 1700 to 1.25 million in 1750.

Britain came to win the war, but at a heavy financial cost. The British treasury had spent seventy million pounds over the course of the fighting, which nearly doubled England's national debt. Furthermore, battles with the French in India had badly damaged Britain's East India Trading Company, an international shipping merchant that nearly collapsed from lack of profit during the war. Because the colonies were both the object of the war with France as well as the primary beneficiaries of Britain's ultimate victory, the British government believed that the American colonists should bear the burden of financing the war. Parliament agreed that new taxes could be leveraged against the colonies. Throughout this period, Parliament hosted no representatives from any of the colonies, making every Act that Parliament passed regarding the colonies completely unilateral.

was passed in 1733. The Sugar Act, interestingly, actually lowered the tax on molasses. The Sugar Act did, however, expand the scope of taxed commodities, including coffee and certain wines.

Because American merchants largely avoided having to pay any duty on sugar and molasses under the original act due to corruption, the Sugar Act also introduced stricter means of enforcement to ensure the colonies were paying their taxes. Among these measures was an expanded naval presence with the directive to more actively pursue customs violations, such as smuggling. British ships were now permitted to board colonial merchant ships based on suspicion alone. London began issuing "writs of assistance," documents that permitted ships in the royal navy to board and search colonial vessels, as well as to seize contraband and prosecute offenders.

New taxes such as the Sugar Act and, later, the Stamp Act were not the only financial concern of the colonies in the years following the Revolution. The French and Indian War also had economic consequences for the colonies, which had been thrown into a depression when the fighting stopped. Many colonial merchants, including the patriot John Hancock's brother, were forced out of business. In Philadelphia, the merchant house of Bayton, Wharton, and Morgan, one of the largest of its kind in the colonies, collapsed. When it did, it held £94,000 in liabilities. Historian Gary B. Nash likens the fall of Bayton, Wharton, and Morgan to the 2001 collapse of Enron, which at the time was the seventh-largest company in the United States and signaled the beginning of a severe economic downturn.

The American colonists directed their accusations across the Atlantic to Britain. The colonial economy was maturing, with skilled craftsmen producing finished merchandise and the overall market diversifying. However, Britain was still holding onto an economic model that had been in place since the first Europeans arrived in the New World, where merchandise and commodities only flowed one-way. Under this outdated system, the North American colonies produced food and raw materials, such as rice, tobacco, lumber, which were shipped to England by English merchants; England, meanwhile, made finished goods, such as cigarettes and furniture, which were imported into the colonies. This circular trade primarily benefited English craftsmen and merchants, who profited from their preferential standing in the system. The way the system was set up, the colonies existed to supply Britain with the materials needed to make Britain wealthy and powerful. Meanwhile, the colonies, which depended on British merchants and bankers to finance their participation in a British-oriented system, were being sucked dry.

As the writings of Enlightenment philosophers encouraging people to rethink such long-held institutions such as the British monarchy spread, the colonists began to see themselves as taking part in one of the many struggles for liberty that had occurred throughout the history of Great Britain. The colonists were, after all, descendants of British ancestors who had fought in such conflicts as the English Civil War, which pitted monarchists against parliamentarians in a battle for more equal distribution of power between the king and the people. Now, with stifled economic development and increasingly frequent imposition of taxes without Parliamentary representation, many colonists imagined that a new era of rebellion was needed.

Tensions Rise in Boston

Although the acts passed by Parliament in the wake of the French and Indian War affected residents in every colony, the capital of the Massachusetts Bay colony, Boston, was especially hard hit. Boston had been the most populous city in the colonies up until the 1750s, boasting a population of over fifteen thousand. It also featured an excellent natural harbor, which made it the busiest port in North America and, in fact, the third busiest port in the whole British Empire (following London and Bristol, both located in England).

Boston's geographical characteristics made it an ideal place for the British to establish a protective garrison in the wake of the French and Indian War. In the eighteenth century, Boston was connected to the Massachusetts mainland only by the Shawmut peninsula, which flooded during high tide, turning the city into an island. Physically isolated for half the day and surrounded by water, Boston could be easily manned by a relatively small force of four thousand soldiers and protected by the legendary Royal Navy. Ironically, this protective garrison only helped to antagonize revolutionary sentiment in the city.

Although Massachusetts was not the oldest British colony in North America, Boston's storied history played a large part in establishing its reputation as the powder keg for the American Revolution. Massachusetts was founded in the 1620s by settlers known as Puritans, who originally came from England. Also known as the Pilgrims, the Puritans were believers in a fundamentalist version of Christianity that prized authentic devotion to God through a strict and simple lifestyle. Puritans in England frequently criticized members of other religions, including even the king, who was the head of the Church of England. Their unusual lifestyle and outspokenness made them unpopular in England, and the Puritans were quickly targeted for persecution.

The Puritans traveled to the New World in search of the freedom to practice their religion the way they saw fit, ultimately landing in Massachusetts Bay. There, they established Plymouth, located approximately 40 miles (64 kilometers) south of Boston. Unlike most other colonists, those who settled in Massachusetts saw themselves as neither culturally nor relationally British; indeed, their existence in the New World was a consequence of alienation at the hands of the **Crown**, a fact that people in Massachusetts kept in mind for generations after settling. Given this mindset, it is no wonder that the **loyalist** Peter Oliver, the Chief Justice of Massachusetts' Superior Court and supporter of the British throughout the revolution, referred to Boston as the "Metropolis of Sedition."

Massachusetts generally and Boston in particular became the center for rebels, who considered the soldiers stationed in their colony to be an invasion and the acts passed by Parliament to be "as blank piece[s] of paper and not more." Among these acts was

Place to affix the STAMP

Hereabouts will be the

Many Americans were furious over the Stamp Act. This political cartoon from a colonial newspaper suggests that many Americans would rather die than pay the hated tax.

the Stamp Act. Passed in 1756, the Stamp Act imposed a duty on a variety of documents marked with a stamp, including newspapers, legal and business documents, licenses, and playing cards.

The colonists reacted strongly to the taxes that were associated with the Stamp Act, which were among the first of their kind. Up until this point, Parliamentary taxes were primarily enacted to regulate commerce; for the first time, Parliament passed an act whose primary objective was to raise money through a direct tax on colonists. Furthermore, as with the Sugar Act, the Stamp Act changed the nature of legal prosecution for those suspected of violating the law. Those accused of undermining the Stamp Act could be tried in what were known as vice-admiralty courts, which did not feature juries—a right that the colonists, as British citizens, had come to expect.

As a result of the Stamp Act, colonists throughout North America began boycotting British goods. Violent protests sprang up, especially in Boston, where a group known as the Sons of Liberty

Revolutionary sentiment was strongest in Boston, the colonial capital of Massachusetts, where protests of angry citizens hoisting effigies of despised royal officials were common.

wrought havoc on those fellow colonists who harbored loyalist sentiments. The Sons of Liberty vandalized loyalist storefronts and encouraged colonists to boycott those businesses. One night, the Sons of Liberty recruited a mob of Bostonians, who marched through the streets holding an **effigy** of Boston's royal stamp distributor, Andrew Oliver. When the mob arrived at what was known as Liberty Tree, they hung the effigy by the neck, beheaded it, and then proceeded to pillage Oliver's home. Boston's dissent did not end there. Smugglers based out of the city engaged in an extensive campaign of smuggling that dramatically hurt Britain's economic advantage in the colonies.

Parliament repealed the Stamp Act in 1766, but passed the Townshend Revenue Act shortly after. The Townshend Act placed taxes on glass, paint, oil, lead, paper, and tea. Parliament estimated that the revenues from the act would raise forty thousand pounds per year, which would go toward the costs associated with administering the colonies. Just as with the Stamp Act, the American colonists resented the imposition on their affairs. To combat the act, Boston smugglers started importing illegal tea, which weakened the legitimate British merchants who were required by law to honor the trade regulations established by Parliament. Mobs of colonists would wait at docks and turn away ships carrying British tea on threat of physical force. Thanks to colonial smuggling operations, the Townshend Act only raised £21,000—about half of the amount the British government expected.

Bloodshed in Boston

Throughout this time, mobs in Boston grew larger and more belligerent, and the British soldiers stationed in the city were set increasingly on edge. Over the winter of 1770, the colonists' frustration and the anxiety of the British culminated in bloodshed. On February 22, a British customs enforcer named Ebenezer Richardson shot and killed Christopher Seider. Seider had joined a group of Bostonians who harassed Richardson for collecting duties for the British. Seider, who was only eleven years old, quickly became a martyr for the patriots. Clashes between the patriots and the British grew in intensity and frequency, breaking out in nearly every corner of the city.

On March 22, a group of young Bostonians started harassing a British watchman stationed outside of the Boston Customs House. As Captain Thomas Preston ordered seven other soldiers to reinforce the lone watchman, the crowd swelled into a mob. The patriots started jeering at them and throwing snowballs and stones at the British soldiers. At some point during the riot, a shot was

Patriot Paul Revere's engraving of what became known as the Boston Massacre took some liberties in depicting the event. It helped to fuel America's drive toward independence.

fired. It is not known if it came from one of the British soldiers, who were under orders not to fire their weapons, or from one of the patriots. After the shot, British soldiers opened fire into the crowd, instantly killing three civilians: Samuel Gray, Crispus Attucks, and James Caldwell. Samuel Maverick and Patrick Carr, who had been wounded in the riot, also later died as a result of their wounds.

The colonists and the British blamed each other for the deaths that night. Although questions remain to this day as to which side fired first, the British believed the tragedy could have been avoided had the colonists not taken such a contentious stance toward acts of Parliament in the first place. The colonists, meanwhile, fought back, labeling the event the "Boston Massacre." The patriot Paul Revere made an engraving titled "The Bloody Massacre perpetrated in King Street," which depicted an organized line of British soldiers, called redcoats, under the command of a superior officer opening fire into a crowd of unarmed, frightened, and retreating colonists. Although Revere's engraving took many liberties in sensationalizing the event, color prints sold like wildfire. Soon, nearly everyone in the colonies had heard about the Boston Massacre.

The Boston Tea Party

In May of 1773, Parliament passed a law known as the Tea Act to support the East India Company. Parliament granted the East India Company a monopoly, giving it the right to all tea trade in the North American colonies. Although there would still be a tax on the tea, without having to compete with other merchants, the East India Company could sell tea for less than what even smugglers were charging. Great Britain's Prime Minister, Lord Frederick North, who conceived of the idea, hoped that the solution would make everyone happy. The East India Company would be saved from financial collapse, the colonists would be pacified with less expensive tea, and the British government would raise the needed tax revenue.

While Lord North's plan made perfect economic sense, he failed to account for one thing: the fury of the colonists, which did not subscribe to the same reason as market economics. The point, the colonists thought, was not that taxed goods were more expensive than they had been when they were not taxed; the colonists were upset over the enactment of taxes by a Parliament that did not also include representatives from the North American colonies. What

On December 16, 1773, the Sons of Liberty boarded British merchant ships docked in Boston harbor and dumped thousands of pounds' worth of tea into the sea. British response to the Boston Tea Party was swift, shutting down the harbor and enforcing martial law on the city.

Lord North had hoped would defuse the tension only sent the colonists—and in particular the residents of Boston—into a frenzy. The "tea crisis," as it became known, marked the dramatic escalation of tensions between the colonies and the mother country. While the British wrangled with the issue of solidifying their authority and exacting revenues from Parliament's taxes, the Sons of Liberty held secret meetings about their next plan of action should negotiations with the royal representatives fail.

On the night of December 16, 1773, the Sons of Liberty, led by a local brewer and tavern keeper named Samuel Adams, boarded the *Beaver*, the *Dartmouth*, and the *Eleanor*, three British East India Company merchant ships docked in the Boston harbor. Over the course of the night, the colonists destroyed 340 chests of tea by throwing them into the harbor. The tea weighed 92,000 pounds (41,730 kilograms) and was valued at £9,659, which would amount to over $1.7 million in today's money.

The Intolerable Acts

Great Britain's response to news of the insurrection in Boston was severe. Through a series of measures known to colonists as both the Intolerable Acts and the Coercive Acts, Great Britain began a concentrated campaign to beat the colonists into submission, with special attention placed on Boston. In early 1774, under the Massachusetts Government Act, Massachusetts' royal governor, Thomas Hutchinson, who had become the object of hatred among Bostonians for his loyalist tendencies, was replaced by General Thomas Gage. Gage was a veteran of the French and Indian Wars, and his arrival in Boston began a period of military government in the city.

While Bostonians were glad to see the hated Hutchinson go, Gage quickly made a name for himself in Boston for strictly enforcing the Intolerable Acts. First, Gage saw to it that the port of Boston was closed until the colonists had paid for the destroyed tea. Because the port was so central to life in Boston, many of its residents had made their living in some way associated with it. Once the port was closed, hundreds of merchants, sailors, shipwrights, and laborers were out of work. Gage forbade the colonists from organizing town councils and meetings, which had been a common feature of daily life in Massachusetts since its founding. Furthermore, under the Administration of Justice Act, British officials who had been charged with capital offenses in the colonies were permitted to go to England or another colony for trial, thereby escaping colonial retribution.

To the people of Boston, the Intolerable Acts constituted an unprecedented interference in their affairs and self-determination. Without work, a public space to air grievances, and justice to prosecute British officials as they saw fit, the colonists in Massachusetts felt completely **disenfranchised**.

Jefferson: A Natural Revolutionary

As the events in Massachusetts unfolded, Thomas Jefferson, like many of his contemporaries, felt that more serious steps were necessary to assert the rights of the colonists in the face of British tyranny. With his election to the Virginia House of Burgesses in 1768 as a representative of Albemarle County, Thomas Jefferson was poised to begin his public career at the start of one of the most pivotal moments in history.

Since his birth, it seems that Jefferson was destined to become one of the leaders of the budding revolution, in large part because of his upbringing as a Virginian. Virginia was perhaps second only to Massachusetts for having the right circumstances to foment discontent with the British. Virginia became the first British colony in North America with the founding of the first permanent settlement at Jamestown in 1607, which replaced the failed colony at Roanoke, Virginia, whose inhabitants mysteriously disappeared in the late 1580s. This historical legacy led Virginians to expect a certain respect owed to them, particularly from their British brothers across the Atlantic.

Virginia was also the most populous of the British colonies in North America at the time, claiming nearly double the population of the second-most populous colony, Pennsylvania, and nearly a quarter of the overall population. Virginians, however, owed a disproportionate amount to British **creditors**—£2.3 million, which was almost half of the debt owed by all the colonies. These debts were hereditary. Fathers who had borrowed heavily to finance tobacco farms passed their debts on to their sons, who struggled to make the payments. These financial burdens on Virginians had two effects: First, it fueled resentment toward the faceless British creditors living on the opposite side of the ocean who collected debt payments; second, it motivated wealthy Virginia planters who had borrowed heavily in the past to seek ways to sever the colony's ties with Great Britain.

Thomas Jefferson, like many other aristocratic Virginians, was subjected to the harsh financial realities of owing money to British merchants. When Jefferson's father-in-law, John Wayles, died in 1773, the estate was heavily indebted. Wayles still owed eleven thousand pounds at the time of this death. When Jefferson divided the estate between himself and Wayles's two other sons-in-law, Wayles's debt was extended to cover Jefferson's own personal property. Jefferson had to sell off much of the inherited land to cover the obligation. In May 1774, Thomas Jefferson and Patrick Henry proposed suspending payments on these hereditary debts in the Virginia House of Burgesses.

There were additional consequences to this extraordinary debt owed by Virginians. The British Parliament had passed a law that restricted the settlement of new lands to the west of Virginia, which many Virginians considered to be their birthright. British rule mandated that only those with capital or those capable of borrowing were permitted to settle there. Because of the rampant debt, very few Virginians could muster the funds to settle in the west.

These factors—Virginia's unique historical legacy, the financial hardship of hereditary debt held by British creditors, and harsh restrictions placed on settlement and expansion—conspired to make Virginia one of the most receptive colonies to the idea of independence from Great Britain. Independence, many thought, would solve all problems, granting Virginians the liberty and autonomy they desired to claim their place in the world.

British Intrusion on Virginian Affairs

Lack of national determination and economic disadvantages were not the only source of anger that the American colonists felt. While

Parliament legislated the British Empire as it always did, it seemed to many colonists that the royal government was trying to expand its influence on domestic affairs. Virginians in particular were growing increasingly frustrated at the royal governor, who had begun clamping down on the colonial government in the years leading up to the Revolution. Before 1729, the colonial legislature had never had one of its laws overturned by the governor. But from 1729 until 1764, the governor suspended nearly sixty laws passed by the colonial government. Between 1764 and 1773—a span of just nine years—the governor intervened more times than he had during the thirty-five previous years, an exceptional seventy-five times. Given this exponential growth of royal intervention on what the colonists saw as their affairs, it's no wonder that Virginians started to worry that what little autonomy had been granted them by the British Empire was starting to slip away.

As Jefferson and other Virginians heard the news out of Boston, they grew infuriated. What was happening in the North was similar to what was happening in their home colony, though on a much more severe scale. Boston became the rallying cry to those Virginians who thought that the revolutionaries could at last reconcile their complaints with the Crown. Discontent, Boston proved, would be met only with force on the part of the British. During a meeting with the House of Burgesses, Jefferson declared, "we must boldly take an unequivocal stand in the line with Massachusetts." Many of his colleagues agreed.

Lexington and Concord

In February of 1775, Parliament formally declared Massachusetts to be in a state of rebellion. When word reached General Gage, King George III asked him to take steps to quash the uprising. The king ordered Gage to march on Concord, a small town located 20 miles (32 km) from Boston, where the Massachusetts colonial militia had stored weapons, gunpowder, and other supplies for an army of

British regulars and American militiamen exchanged gunfire at the towns of Lexington and Concord, Massachusetts, officially marking the beginning of the American Revolution.

14,000 militiamen. Gage was also to head toward Lexington, which neighbored Concord, and arrest the patriot leaders Samuel Adams and John Hancock, among others.

Gage planned the assault under the utmost secrecy, but news still reached the colonial militia. On April 18, Dr. Joseph Warren, a patriot, received word that the British were planning to attack

Lexington and Concord the following day. Warren sent out Paul Revere and William Dawes to warn the militia there, resulting in the famous "midnight ride." (Contrary to popular belief, Paul Revere did not speed through the Massachusetts countryside shouting, "The British are coming!" Because the purpose of the ride was to warn the militia so that they could covertly move their weapons and prepare for attack, Revere actually went door to door as quietly as he could.)

On April 19, 1775, approximately seven hundred redcoats marched into Lexington, where they encountered about a tenth as many militiamen in the town square. A British officer commanded the outnumbered militia to disperse. Just as they were about to flee, a shot rang out. The militia and the redcoats exchanged several rounds of fire before the militiamen retreated, allowing the British to continue onto Concord. In the meantime, two thousand colonial militiamen had organized to repel the attack. After several hours of fighting over a constantly shifting front, 273 British and 95 Americans were dead. As with the Boston Massacre, both sides were fueled with rage at the other. "A frenzy of revenge seems to have seized all ranks of people," Jefferson wrote, observing that there was now no longer any hope of reconciling with the British. The revolution had begun in earnest.

CHAPTER THREE

Declaring Independence

The battles of Lexington and Concord began the war, but tensions had been increasing for quite some time. Following the passage of the Intolerable Acts, the revolutionary movement in the American colonies started to gain substantial momentum. Much like General Gage was doing in Boston, royal governors up and down the American coast began tightening their grip on the colonies; however, as if they were holding a handful of sand, the tighter the British clenched, the more the situation started to slip from their fingers. More frequent displays of authority only fortified the belief among colonists that the British were interested in total domination, thus pushing more colonists to the side of the revolutionaries.

Jefferson (*right*), working with input from his editors, John Adams (*center*) and Dr. Benjamin Franklin (*left*), was tasked with drafting the Declaration of Independence.

Popular opinion among the colonists remained relatively split on the matter of independence, however. With the possible exception of most Massachusetts residents, many colonists identified as British subjects, descended from British ancestors and with family members still in Britain. This ironically fueled in the colonists both frustration at the mother country for their treatment and also reluctance to formally separate from Great Britain.

Colonists living in the Mid-Atlantic colonies (including New York, Pennsylvania, Delaware, Maryland, and Virginia) and in the southern colonies were especially susceptible to loyalist tendencies, causing the Boston lawyer and statesman John Adams to declare, "The idea of independence is as unpopular in Pennsylvania and in all the Middle and Southern States as the Stamp Act itself. No man dares to speak it." Those colonists that saw separation from Great Britain as a political necessity, including Thomas Jefferson, were tasked with inspiring their less certain countrymen of the fact. "We were under conviction of the necessity of arousing our people from the lethargy into which they had fallen as to passing events," Jefferson wrote. The country was in need of a wakeup call.

When news of the Boston Port Act, one of the Coercive Acts that restricted trade in Boston harbor, reached Virginia, the House of Burgesses passed the Day of Fasting and Prayer **Resolution** of Tuesday, May 24, 1774. Organized largely by Jefferson, along with the other Burgesses Patrick Henry and Richard Henry Lee, the resolution was among the first official censures of the British by a colony-wide governing organization. On that day, the House of Burgesses encouraged the citizens of Virginia to pray for deliverance from "the evils of civil war," suggesting that if there was to be war, it would be the result of British aggression on a pious colonial people. The Day of Fasting and Prayer was intended to be a wake up call for all those Virginians who had so far been ambivalent to or against the notion of revolution.

The Rights of the Colonies: Jefferson's *Summary View*

On September 5, 1774, four months after the Day of Fasting and Prayer resolution and five months before the battle at Lexington and Concord, delegates from each of the British colonies were called to meet in Philadelphia, Pennsylvania, to discuss the colonial reaction to British intrusion in their affairs. Over the past few years, Jefferson had risen in prominence among his constituents both in Albemarle County as well as in Virginia as a whole as a supporter of the rights of the colonists. Over the summer, Jefferson worked diligently on a document he would present to the Virginia delegates attending the first Continental Congress. When Jefferson finished, he had written more than 6,700 words on liberty in the colonies. Jefferson's paper, titled *A Summary View of the Rights of British America*, was the first of his longer state papers. Jefferson's *Summary View* was a stalwart defense of the rights owed to the colonists. Echoes of the *Summary View* can be found in the Declaration of Independence; together, they illustrate the evolution of Jefferson's philosophy of liberty.

As descendants of British ancestors, Jefferson wrote, the colonists are part of the long history of Great Britain: "Our ancestors, before their emigration to America, were the free inhabitants of the British dominion in Europe, and possessed a right which nature has given to all men, of departing from the country in which chance, not choice, has placed them." As such, reconciliation was preferred in the colonies over independence: "It is neither our wish nor our interest to separate from [Great Britain]." However, Jefferson concluded his paper with a warning for King George III: "Still less let it be proposed that our properties within our own territories shall be taxed or regulated by any power on earth but our own. The God who gave us life gave us liberty at the same time; the hand of force may destroy but cannot disjoin them."

Just as he had done with the Day of Fasting and Prayer, Jefferson had cast the revolution in the least favorable light for the British.

A
SUMMARY VIEW
OF THE
RIGHTS
OF
BRITISH AMERICA.

Set forth in some
RESOLUTIONS
INTENDED FOR
The INSPECTION of the prefent DELEGATES of the People of VIRGINIA, now in CONVENTION.

It is the indifpenfable duty of the fupreme magiftrate to confider himfelf as acting for the whole community, and obliged to fupport its dignity, and affign to the people, with juftice, their various rights, as he would be faithful to the great truft repofed in him.

CICERO's OF. B. 1.

By a NATIVE, and Member of the Houfe of Burgeffes.

Tho Jefferson

WILLIAMSBURG, Printed by CLEMENTINA RIND.

LONDON,
Re-printed for G. KEARSLY, at No. 46, near Serjeants Inn, in Fleet Street, 1774.

Jefferson's first official state paper, *A Summary View of the Rights of British America*, was widely circulated throughout the colonies and earned him the attention and respect of many revolutionaries.

Whereas the Day of Fasting and Prayer had made the colonists out to be pious and respectable dissenters in the face of British tyranny, the *Summary View* made it seem like the British were seeking to destroy their own citizens.

Jefferson gave his *Summary View* to Jupiter, his personal servant, to deliver to Williamsburg because he had fallen ill. Shortly after Jupiter reached Williamsburg, local printer Clementia Rind got ahold of it and began running copies. Inspired by Jefferson's message, Rind wrote in a preface to *Summary View* that she was publishing it without Jefferson's knowledge, but that the people of the colonies had a right to read Jefferson's opinion on the subject. She also attached a quote from the ancient statesman Cicero, who had a reputation for defending liberty in the Roman Republic in the midst of growing conspiracies to reinstitute monarchy: "It is the indispensable duty of the supreme magistrate to consider himself as acting for the whole community, and obliged to support its dignity, and assign to the people, with justice, their various rights, as he would be faithful to the great trust reposed in him."

Jefferson's sentiments contained in his *Summary View* were considered to be quite radical for a Virginian at the time. "Tamer sentiments were preferred, and I believe, wisely preferred; the leap I proposed being too long as yet for the mass of our citizens," Jefferson wrote. However, Jefferson had made a name for himself among revolutionary circles. George Washington himself remarked on reading what he called "Mr. Jefferson's Bill of Rights." Jefferson's paper also earned him the attention of the British. It was rumored that Jefferson was added to a bill of attainder, a document that labeled him guilty of the capital offense of treason.

The Revolution Reaches Virginia

Although the British had not yet occupied Virginia the same way as they had Boston, tensions were still growing between the colonists there and the royal establishment. The new governor of Virginia, a Scotsman named John Murray, the Fourth Earl of Dunmore, took a hardline approach toward the brewing insurrection. Dunmore instituted a ban on imported weapons and powder from Britain, acting on an order from London requiring the seizure of any arms that arrived in America. Furthermore, London also directed its representatives in North America to prevent the elections of representatives to colonial congresses.

In March 1775, Jefferson traveled to the Anglican Church of St. John's, where revolutionaries like himself were hosting the Virginia Convention. St. John's was chosen as it was the largest structure in Richmond, and organizers estimated that around a hundred people would attend. That number turned out to be a vast underestimation. The inside pews were packed with representatives and spectators, with many more standing outside listening through open windows.

At the Virginia Convention, Jefferson and the other delegates busied themselves with matters of war: organizing the militia, raising revenue, and continuing trade. It was at the Virginia Convention that Patrick Henry, one of Jefferson's political icons, implored his colleagues to take a defensive military posture. "Gentleman may cry, Peace, Peace," Henry said. "But there is no peace. The war is actually begun! … I know now what course others may take; but as for me—give me liberty, or give me death!" Just as the British stepped up efforts to quash the insurrection, Jefferson and the Virginian delegates were preparing for the likelihood of war.

However, it was not only war from without that the Virginia Convention delegates were concerned about. War from within, in the form of slave revolts, was just as real a worry to Virginians as a

British invasion. In mid-April, two slaves in Chesterfield County set fire to a militia officer's house. When word spread to the neighboring counties, white Virginians grew fearful that a widespread slave rebellion was on the horizon.

In colonies where slaves comprised a large part of the population, such as Virginia, many royal officials threatened to free the slaves and arm them against the revolutionaries.

Disarming the Revolutionaries

One of the great fears of the royal establishment in the colonies was that other Americans would take up arms against the British as the people of Massachusetts had. In the hopes of heading off an armed uprising, many governors, including Virginia's, took measures to disarm the colonists just as General Gage had done in Boston.

On April 21, 1775, Governor Dunmore seized the powder magazine at Williamsburg and removed it offshore to the Royal Navy ship, the HMS *Magdalen*. Virginians were outraged. Without gunpowder, they would be at a disadvantage to repel a slave rebellion, which was a real possibility. Dunmore had said to a crowd of protestors gathered outside his mansion that the seizure of the magazine was a precautionary measure: In the event of a slave uprising, Dunmore explained, it would be better to remove the possibility of an armed rebellion. However, Dunmore's halfhearted attempt to conceal his true motive did not pacify the protestors for long.

The next day, Dunmore arrested two of the protestors' leaders. On Saturday, April 22, Dunmore said that he would free the slaves and "reduce the city of Williamsburg to ashes" if there were any more moves against the Crown. Later that year, on November 7, Dunmore made good on his threat. From a cabin aboard the HMS *Magdalen*, stationed in the port of Norfolk, Dunmore declared **martial law** in Virginia, and offered any slave or indentured servant freedom if they raised arms against the American rebels.

The Second Continental Congress

Between martial law declared in Boston, open fighting in Massachusetts, skirmishes with the British over gunpowder, and scare tactics by the Virginia royal governor centered on arming slaves against revolutionaries, the colonies seemed to be barreling toward an independence movement. Jefferson wrote, "Nobody now entertains a doubt but that we are able to cope with the whole force of Great Britain if we are but willing to exert ourselves."

With the situation between Britain and the colonies worsening, a second Continental Congress was convened in the summer of 1775. This time, Jefferson himself would be in attendance. Here, in the Pennsylvania State House (later known as Independence Hall), Jefferson threw himself into his work. He reported back to Virginia on the military events taking place in Massachusetts and conferred with the Pennsylvania delegate, Dr. Benjamin Franklin, who had drafted the **Articles of Confederation**, a proposal to establish a unified colonial government in the event of independence. The other colleagues at the Congress took note of the young delegate from Virginia. Rhode Island representative Samuel Ward noted seeing "the famous Mr. Jefferson," whom he recognized from reading the *Summary View*. Jefferson was a celebrity.

Jefferson also spent a lot of his time in Philadelphia meeting delegates from New England, including John Adams. Although the two were different in nearly every way, they made a dynamic pair. Adams was the heat, and Jefferson was the light. A fiery New Englander, the elder, shorter Adams was hot-blooded and struggled to keep his temper in check; Jefferson, meanwhile, taller and younger, was thoughtful and reserved. Despite their differences, Adams and Jefferson worked closely together. Adams' colleague from Massachusetts, Benjamin Rush, wrote in a letter to Adams after the Revolution, "I consider you and him [Jefferson] as the North and South Poles of the American Revolution. Some talked, some wrote, and some fought to promote and establish it, but you and Mr. Jefferson *thought* for us all." Without the cooperation between Adams and Jefferson, independence for America may have been only a fleeting thought during the summer of 1775.

John Adams of Massachusetts proved an invaluable ally to Jefferson in the Second Continental Congress. Working largely behind the scenes, he played a pivotal role in pushing America toward independence.

A Man for the Job

At the start of June 1776, Virginia delegate Richard Henry Lee made a riotous motion on the floor of the Second Continental Congress: that the colonies dissolve "all allegiance to the British Crown." For the first time, independence was no longer the subject of fireside debates and backroom whispers; it was on the table as a political possibility. Debate on the issue was scheduled for the next day.

Reflecting the state of the colonies at the time, the delegates were still split on the matter. Massachusetts and Virginia, who had so far been the hardest hit by British encroachment, led the group of colonies in favor of independence. However, as Adams and his colleagues from Massachusetts previously observed, the middle colonies were still hesitant about seceding from Great Britain. States like New York, Delaware, and even Pennsylvania, where the Congress was being held, had the highest number of loyalists in the colonies; furthermore, these colonies had not had the same experience as Massachusetts and Virginia. With few to no slaves to be threatened by an uprising within the colonies and a population that largely identified as British, these colonies were suspicious of the independence movement.

Unity of the colonies was essential; without each of them on board, the American independence movement would be doomed from the start. Jefferson noted that a fractured America would either prevent foreign powers such as France from joining as allies or lead foreign powers to prop up the cause to such a degree that the Americans would find themselves subject to yet another tyrant.

In order to allow time to convince the other colonies of the prudence of independence, the official vote was delayed three weeks. In the meantime, Congress formed committees to prepare a framework for government among the colonies, a **treaty** to request assistance from France, and a formal declaration of independence, so that Congress could immediately turn its attention to the revolution once the vote was decided.

In declaring independence from Great Britain, there was a larger issue of determining the new nation's place in the world. Up until this point, the colonies had been in service to their mother country; their existence was similar to that of a planet orbiting the sun, drawing sustenance from its heat. Severing the bond that had lasted for over a century meant that the colonies now had to construct their own national identity. They would no longer be British subjects, and they would no longer enjoy the benefits of British citizenship into which they were born. As the united colonies, they were faced with the question of who they were going to be as a new nation of people. This opportunity to start from scratch required the American colonists to invent a nation on their own terms.

This task was both exhilarating and daunting because wrapped up in it was a variety of politically existential questions: Where does a nation come from? What is a nation? What values should a nation uphold? These were monumental questions for a monumental time. The task of initiating the separation and thereby establishing the ideal of America itself fell to the members of the Second Continental Congress, who looked to select one of their own to carry the burden of articulating the unspoken ideals of a new nation.

For John Adams and the other delegates from Massachusetts, the vote on independence and the formation of a committee to draft a formal declaration were the pinnacle of a years-long strategy to sever ties between Great Britain and the colonies. The people of Massachusetts had been prepared for independence for a long time. Their capital had been occupied by British troops and placed under martial law, their port—their livelihood—had been closed off from the world, and the Massachusetts militia had lost men at Lexington and Concord. However, Adams understood the importance of unifying the colonies, and knew that being too forthright on the issue too soon could sour the idea in the minds of other colonists.

The Massachusetts delegates understood that independence would require a long-game approach, and they recognized the political necessity of leading from behind. Rather than steamroll the other delegates in the Continental Congress and risk turning the other colonies off, Adams and his colleagues planned to recruit Virginia to be the face of independence. "You know Virginia is the most populous State in the Union," Adams wrote, recalling a conversation he had with his colleagues. "They are very proud of their ancient dominion, they call it; they think they have a right to take the lead, and the Southern and Middle States, too, are too much disposed to yield it to them." From the beginning, the Massachusetts delegates knew a Virginian should draft the declaration, but which one? John Adams thought his friend, Thomas Jefferson, who was only thirty-three years old at the time, should do it.

Jefferson had experience in articulating the revolutionary sentiments of an oppressed people. The Day of Fasting and Prayer Resolution as well as the *Summary View* were familiar to Adams and the other delegates of the Congress. Jefferson had "a reputation for literature, science, and a happy talent of composition," and his writings had a "peculiar felicity of expression," as Adams explained in a letter to a friend. When the delegates voted on the matter of heading up the committee to draft the declaration, Adams voted for Jefferson. In the end, Jefferson won the most votes, with Adams coming in second. The two were put in charge of the declaration, but Jefferson suggested to Adams that he write it. Adams declined, saying that "I am obnoxious, suspected, and unpopular," and that Jefferson could "write ten times better than I can." The matter was settled. Jefferson began working on the declaration, with Adams as well as Benjamin Franklin working as his editors.

The Declaration of Independence

Jefferson started writing the declaration at the home of Jacob Graff Jr., a prominent Philadelphia bricklayer whose house was located just two blocks from the Pennsylvania State House. Jefferson slept in one room upstairs and wrote in a private parlor at the opposite end of the hall. Over the course of three weeks, Jefferson worked diligently at a small wooden desk that he had designed, writing late into the evenings while his servant, Jupiter, brought him cups of tea. Before this point, Jefferson had thought carefully about independence, and he understood his task well: "Not to find out new principles, or new arguments, never before thought of ... but to place before mankind the common sense of the subject; in terms so plain and firm as to command their assent, and to justify ourselves in the independent stand we were compelled to take."

Perhaps thinking back to Dr. Small's instruction in philosophy, Jefferson drew heavily from the Enlightenment: the Englishman John Locke (1632–1704), the French Baron Montesquieu (1689–1755), as well as many leading thinkers of the Scottish Enlightenment. To Jefferson, the words flowed naturally:

> When in the Course of human events, it becomes necessary for one people to dissolve the political bands which have connected them with another, and to assume among the powers of the earth, the separate and equal station to which the Laws of Nature and of Nature's God entitle them, a decent respect to the opinions of mankind requires that they should declare the causes which impel them to the separation.
>
> We hold these truths to be self-evident, that all men are created equal, that they are endowed by their Creator with certain unalienable Rights, that among these are Life, Liberty and the pursuit of Happiness.—That to secure these rights, Governments are instituted among Men, deriving their just powers from the consent of the governed, —That whenever any Form of Government becomes destructive of these ends, it is the Right of the People to alter or to abolish it, and to institute new

The fifty-six signers of the Declaration of Independence knew they were committing treason, but they were willing to sacrifice everything for the goal of a free America.

Government, laying its foundation on such principles and organizing its powers in such form, as to them shall seem most likely to effect their Safety and Happiness. Prudence, indeed, will dictate that Governments long established should not be changed for light and transient causes; and accordingly all experience hath shewn, that mankind are more disposed to suffer, while evils are sufferable, than to right themselves by abolishing the forms to which they are accustomed. But when a long train of abuses and usurpations, pursuing invariably the same Object evinces a design to reduce them under absolute Despotism, it is their right, it is their duty, to throw off such Government, and to provide new Guards for their future security.— Such has been the patient sufferance of these Colonies; and such is now the necessity which constrains them to alter their former Systems of Government. The history of the present King of Great Britain is a history of repeated injuries and usurpations, all having in direct object the establishment of an absolute Tyranny over these States. To prove this, let Facts be submitted to a candid world ...

We, therefore, the Representatives of the united States of America, in General Congress, Assembled, appealing to the Supreme Judge of the world for the rectitude of our intentions, do, in the Name, and by Authority of the good People of these Colonies, solemnly publish and declare, That these United Colonies are, and of Right ought to be Free and Independent States; that they are Absolved from all Allegiance to the British Crown, and that all political connection between them and the State of Great Britain, is and ought to be totally dissolved; and that as Free and Independent States, they have full Power to levy War, conclude Peace, contract Alliances, establish Commerce, and to do all other Acts and Things which Independent States may of right do. And for the

AMERICAN LOYALISTS REACT

Not every person living in the American colonies was on board with declaring independence from Great Britain. Popular opinion was split among everyday Americans, and there were still a number of people who actually supported the British government. These people were known variously as royalists, loyalists, or "Tories" and included everyday colonists as well as royal representatives, such as governors and agents.

The most famous loyalist during the Revolution was Thomas Hutchinson. Born in Boston, Massachusetts, in 1711, Hutchinson served as the royal governor of Massachusetts at the height of pre-revolutionary tension, presiding during both the Boston Massacre and the Boston Tea Party. As a royal appointee, Hutchinson had no patience for the rebels, nor they for him. When Hutchinson publicly declared, "[i]t is better to submit to some abridgment of our rights, than to break off our connection with our protector, England," he became the target of revolutionary spite. In 1765, a Boston mob broke into Hutchinson's mansion, stealing valuables and vandalizing the property.

Following the publication of the Declaration of Independence, Hutchinson wrote *Strictures upon the Declaration of Independence of the Congress at Philadelphia.* In the document, addressed like a letter to King George III, Hutchinson attacks and refutes each point made in the Declaration, as well as justifying the system of government that created the circumstances for revolution. In conclusion, Hutchinson chastises the rebels for refusing to respect the same sort of liberty and freedom of speech that had made Hutchinson and other loyalists targets of revolutionary anger: "under the free government in America, no man may, by writing or speaking, contradict any part of this Declaration, without being deemed an enemy to his country, and exposed to the rage and fury of the populace." Hutchinson was not far from the mark. His outspoken support of the royal government made him a target of many revolutionary protests. Throughout Boston, effigies of Hutchinson made of straw were hanged and burned.

support of this Declaration, with a firm reliance on the protection of divine Providence, we mutually pledge to each other our Lives, our Fortunes and our sacred Honor.

As Jefferson wrote, he kept in his mind the magnitude of his words. He knew full well what he was doing, and he considered his language to be practically **sacrosanct**. "Politics as well as religion has its superstitions," Jefferson later said, thinking of the desk on which he wrote the declaration: "These gaining strength with time may one day give imaginary value to this relic for its association with the birth of the Great Charter of our Independence." (He wasn't far off: Jefferson's desk is currently on display in the National Museum of American History in Washington, DC, and Jacob Graff's house on 7th Street, known as the "Declaration House," currently enjoys status as a Independence National Historical Park building.)

The declaration was introduced on Friday, June 28, 1776. The delegates were given the weekend to read the document and collect their thoughts, and instructed to return on Monday, July 1, to debate it. Much of Jefferson's original draft was revised, and large parts of it— including reprimands against King George III for institutionalizing slavery in the colonies—were deleted. The debate pained Jefferson. When Franklin observed the quiet Jefferson squirming in his chair as he watched the pinnacle of his life's work criticized on the floor, he said, "I have made it a rule, whenever in my power, to avoid becoming the draughtsman of papers to be reviewed by a public body."

The Birth of a Nation

Despite the back and forth, Jefferson had accomplished his task. The delegates agreed to adopt the resolution on Tuesday, July 2. On Thursday, July 4, 1776, they **ratified** it, affixing their signatures to the bottom of the Declaration of Independence. Benjamin Rush, a delegate from Pennsylvania, recalled the event in a letter he wrote to John Adams in 1811:

The Declaration of Independence was read aloud to a crowd of cheering colonists days after it was ratified.

Scarcely a word was said of the solitude and labors and fears and sorrows and sleepless nights of the men who projected, proposed, defended, and subscribed the Declaration of Independence. Do you recollect your memorable speech upon the day on which the vote was taken? Do you recollect the pensive and awful silence which pervaded the house when we were called up, one after another, to the table of the president of Congress to subscribe what was believed by many at that time to be our own death warrants?

Overnight, the local printer John Dunlap ran the Declaration of Independence through his press, creating the first set of published copies. Two days later, the Declaration graced the front page of *The Pennsylvania Evening Post*. Two days after that, the Congress announced the news to a crowd assembled before the State House. When they had finished, they were met with cheers of "God bless the free states of North America."

Copies of the Declaration of Independence fanned out through the colonies. Colonists throughout America celebrated their newfound independence. The Massachusetts reverend Ezra Stiles took on an incredulous tone. Having experienced the tragedies of the Intolerable Acts firsthand, Stiles could hardly believe that he had seen America's moment of independence come:

Thus the Congress has tied a Gordian knot, which the Parl[iament] will find they can neither cut, nor untie. The *thirteen united colonies* now rise into an *Independent Republic* among the kingdoms, states, and empires of earth … And I have lived to see such an important and astonishing revolution?

General George Washington, fresh off the liberation of Boston and preparing for a British invasion of New York at the time, also received a copy. In his General Orders, he recorded his desire to have the declaration read to his men:

> The general hopes this important event will serve as a fresh incentive to every officer and soldier to act with fidelity and courage, as knowing that now the peace and safety of his country depends (under God) solely on the success of our arms: And that he is now in the service of a state possessed of sufficient power to reward his merit, and advance him to the highest honors of a free country.

General Henry Knox, who accompanied George Washington, said, "The eyes of all America are upon us. As we play our part, posterity will bless us or curse us."

By the summer of 1776, the revolution was already raging. The patriot army under General Washington had already liberated Boston from the British and was now under threat of an even larger invasion of redcoats in New York. The Declaration of Independence did not start the hostilities, nor would it end them. However, for the first time, the Americans were no longer simply defending their home, not battling for their rights as Englishmen. The stakes had been raised. Now, the American Revolution was a fight for the ideals of a free and independent nation, one that would be created not from arbitrary boundaries but from gritty self-determination.

CHAPTER FOUR

Jefferson Philosophy in Action

I n the wake of declaring independence, Jefferson left Philadelphia and returned to Virginia. Jefferson served as both a legislator and governor of his home state during the Revolutionary War. During this time, Jefferson refined the lofty ideals he had imbued in the Declaration, working to make the abstractions of "life, liberty, and the pursuit of happiness" political realities for his countrymen. Jefferson had never been content to simply philosophize, as the Declaration of Independence—though a political document—was primarily about the idea of America. Rather, Jefferson also worked tirelessly on actually realizing the more equal world of which he had dreamed. The legislation and other writings he crafted during this time not only illuminated the sort of statesman he desired to be but also helped to provide the foundation for an entire

> Jefferson would get the chance to apply the ideals he expressed in the Declaration of Independence during his political career, which included the offices of governor, secretary of state, and, ultimately, president.

political party—among the first in what would soon be the United States—known as the **Democratic-Republicans**.

Expanding Opportunity in Virginia

In October 1776, Jefferson was selected by the citizens of Virginia to legislate for them as a member of the General Assembly located in Williamsburg. Not one to rest on his laurels, Jefferson embarked on a broad initiative to expand equality and liberty in his home state. He did this primarily through abolishing laws that had been in existence since the founding of the colony back in 1607. Given the colonies' newfound independence from Great Britain, the time was ripe to do away with outdated traditions that continued to link Virginia with the old mother country, culturally if not politically.

Jefferson first went to work dismantling the custom of **primogeniture**, which mandated that landowners pass the entirety of their property to a single heir, typically the first-born son in the family. "Primogeniture" comes from Latin and means "firstborn." Primogeniture had been a part of life in England since the feudal system in the Middle Ages. Under the feudal system, power was linked to property ownership. The king, who held the most power and all the property, distributed his power and property to lords, who in turn allowed peasants known as serfs to work the lord's land in exchange for protection. (The term "landlord" was coined in this system.) Lords recognized the importance of keeping their estates as large and as unified as possible in order to consolidate power over those who worked the land. Primogeniture allowed the lord's land to remain whole when he died. This kept power within the family, but at the expense of upward mobility; because land was transferred as a whole to a single descendant of a family, commoners were not able to marry into property or otherwise acquire a parcel for themselves.

Although Jefferson had himself benefited from primogeniture in Virginia as the firstborn son of his family and inherited a profitable plantation, hundreds of slaves, and thousands of acres of land from his father, he recognized the necessity of upholding the common good by abolishing this practice. Primogeniture also had close associations with Great Britain and the monarchy, who historically used primogeniture to consolidate absolute power. Having just declared independence from Britain, primogeniture was inconsistent with revolutionary ideals of equal access to power and happiness.

Related to Jefferson's interest in broadening access to power through property laws, Jefferson also created a system of public education for white Virginians and hastened the process for foreign-born people living in Virginia to become citizens. Both of these initiatives sought to expand opportunities for Virginians as a whole.

Crusading for Religious Freedom

One facet of liberty that Jefferson had always been keenly protective of was "freedom of conscience," which he considered the right of people to live according to what they thought was best, as long as it didn't negatively affect others. Inspired particularly by the writings of John Locke, Jefferson believed that all humans were born with reason, which allowed individuals to determine the best course for their own lives.

However, during Jefferson's time, Virginia dramatically limited this freedom of conscience. Just as England had done before it, Virginia recognized the Church of England (also known as Anglicanism), a form of Protestant Christianity with roots in the English monarchy, as the official state religion. It was not unusual for nations to officially sanction a particular religion; in fact, it was the norm. Nearly every political body on earth, from the ancient Egyptians to eighteenth-century England, required its citizens to practice a proscribed religion, which helped to bolster national identity and make the task of governing easier.

State religions were not without their problems, however. Protecting an official state religion closely linked civil rights with religious expression at the expense of those who practiced another religion or no religion at all. In England, official protection of Anglicanism resulted in persecution of many different religious sects, including Catholics and Puritans. Members of both groups fled to America in search of the freedom to respect their consciences, settling in Maryland and Massachusetts, respectively. In Virginia, those who did not practice Anglicanism were prevented from serving either in government or the military. Children were required by law to be baptized into the Anglican Church, and in some cases children were taken from their homes if the children's parents did not belong to the religion.

To Jefferson, state religion constituted "spiritual tyranny." Not only did it place citizens of different beliefs on unequal footing, it also directly harmed people's ability to reason. Mandated religious beliefs prevented people from questioning religion, which restricted the God-given right to think for oneself. In order to correct this artifact of British tyranny, Jefferson introduced legislation designed to abolish any mention of religion in state matters in the fall of 1776. Establishing religious liberty in Virginia was an uphill battle, however. Many of his colleagues pushed back against the motion, leading Jefferson to refer to the repeated legislative fights as "the severest contest in which I have ever been engaged."

Over the next several years, Jefferson made incremental steps toward his goal of dismantling Virginia's state religious ordinances. On January 16, 1786, the General Assembly passed the Virginia State for Religious Freedom. Its third paragraph reflected Jefferson's belief in the natural rights of men:

> Be it enacted by the General Assembly, that no man shall be compelled to frequent or support any religious worship, place, or ministry whatsoever, nor shall be enforced, restrained, molested, or burthened in his body or goods, nor shall otherwise suffer on account of his religious opinions or belief; but that all men shall be free to profess, and by argument to maintain, their opinion in matters of religion, and that the same shall in no wise diminish, enlarge, or affect their civil capacities.

Jefferson's efforts to protect religious liberty in Virginia became a defining feature of the larger American political landscape. The Jeffersonian concept of freedom of conscience, especially in regards to matters of religion, even made its way into the Bill of Rights, the list of fundamental freedoms that are guaranteed to all Americans.

Jefferson continued to serve his home state as a representative and then governor until 1781, when he briefly retired from public office. In 1784, he reentered the political field, serving as trade commissioner in France before replacing Ben Franklin as minister.

In 1790, Jefferson became the nation's first secretary of state, accepting the position in the new president George Washington's cabinet. Yet again, Jefferson found himself thrust into the national sphere. As a delegate to the Continental Congress, he was tasked with articulating the ideals of American society; now, he would have the chance to help realize those ideals. Just as he had designed his home at Monticello relatively quickly yet spent decades actually constructing it, the process of actually building a practical framework of government would prove more difficult to Jefferson than conceiving its founding principles.

The New Constitution and the Federalist Party

In the wake of the American Revolution, the United States was originally organized under the Articles of Confederation. First proposed by Ben Franklin, the Articles of Confederation were adopted by the Continental Congress on November 15, 1777. The Articles were flawed from the beginning, however. As a sign of things to come, for example, it took until March 1, 1781—over three years after they were adopted by Congress—for Maryland, the last state, to adopt it themselves.

In the interest of protecting the rights of the states, the Articles only provided for a national legislature to vote and enact laws. However, the national legislature had no power to enforce the laws it passed on the states. Each of the states had their own taxes, tariffs, and currencies, leading to virtual chaos within the nation. The situation exploded when farmers in western Massachusetts who struggled to make debt and tax payments and were threatened with foreclosures rebelled against the state government. Commanded by Revolutionary War captain Daniel Shays, the rebels were soon subdued by a Massachusetts militia, but the discontent spread to neighboring states.

Between the unequal application of law and the threat of populist uprisings like Shays' Rebellion, it became clear that the United States needed a new constitution. In 1787, Congress hosted the Constitutional Convention to develop a new government framework that would more evenly balance states' rights with national power. Under the new constitution, the states would be supervised by a national government consisting of a bicameral (two-house) Congress to pass laws, the Supreme Court to review the justness of the laws passed, and the presidency to enforce the laws and command the military. At last, the United States government had the power and the oversight to effectively control the states.

The debate over a new constitution gave rise to a political group known as the **Federalists**, who favored a strong centralized national government. (The name "federalist" comes from the **federal government**, which is organized at the national level). Many federalists were situated in the Northeast, whose economies were dramatically weakened during the time of the Articles of Confederation. Many people who would become federalists originally called for a new Constitution. The Federalists soon became the world's first organized **political party**. Under the name of Federalists, people cooperated to win elections in order to realize their vision of a strong federal government.

The Federalists did not become clearly defined until the last decade of the eighteenth century when Alexander Hamilton was selected to serve as the nation's first secretary of the treasury in September 1789. Hamilton was tasked by the House of Representatives to address the United States' debt problem and to devise a plan to bolster national

Revolutionary War hero, secretary of the treasury, and leader of the Federalist party, Alexander Hamilton proved one of Jefferson's thorniest political adversaries.

credit. The nation's debt totaled over seventy-nine million dollars. (In 2011, the Congressional Research Service calculated debt from the American Revolution to total nearly $2.5 billion in today's dollars.) Of that total debt, only twelve million dollars was owed to foreign governments; the rest was owed to the American people. This breakdown posed several problems for Hamilton. While the debt owed to foreign governments was well defined and had clear interest calculations, the domestic debt was a tangle of **debtors**, creditors, and interest rates. Both during and after the war, many different agencies within both state governments as well as the Confederation issued a variety of bills, notes, and certificates to cover these debts.

In order to demonstrate to creditors that the United States was a reliable and dependable borrower, Hamilton understood that all foreign debt had to be paid in full; likewise, in order to build faith among the American people that the new federal government was looking out for their interests, all domestic debts had to be dealt with fairly. After diving into the situation and delivering a forty-thousand-word report titled *Report on Public Credit in January 1790*, Hamilton seemed to have a solution.

Hamilton proposed that the national government fund not only its share of the overall debt but also the states' debts as well. By spreading the responsibility for paying the states' debts over the entire country, it would lower the taxes of people in states with higher debt burdens, an issue that had given rise to discontent like Shays' Rebellion. Once the federal government had assumed the states' debts, it would "fund" them, meaning that it would pay the interest on the debts while absorbing the principal (the actual loaned amount) as a relatively permanent debt. This would make creditors happy, because they would have a regular stream of income from the debts, boosting the United States' credit. It would also benefit the United States, Hamilton said, because it would allow the country to keep the money it had taken out while only making minimal interest payments funded through customs duties and excise taxes.

Additionally, Hamilton proposed creating a national bank, the Bank of the United States, which would provide short-term loans to large, well-established merchants. Finally, Hamilton proposed opening a national mint to consolidate all the various currencies circulating in the states at the time.

Hamilton's plan reflected the federalists' desire to push the United States as quickly as possible toward a sophisticated industrial economy supported by large-scale manufacturers capable of supplying the country with everything it needed—in other words, to declare economic independence from the merchants and manufacturers of

LIBERTY AND BANKS

Of Hamilton's proposals, many people—especially southern planters—took special issue with the creation of a national bank. Banks have the power to create money at will, which many farmers consider to be unnatural and unjust.

Banks are required to keep only a fraction of their actual deposits on hand. This is known as a reserve. They are then allowed to loan out the balance between the money people deposit and the reserve, thereby "creating" money. For a simple example of how this works, imagine ten people each deposit one hundred dollars into a bank, making one thousand dollars in overall deposits. However, the bank is only required to keep 10 percent—$100—on hand in case someone wants to withdraw their deposit. The bank may loan out the remaining nine hundred dollars to other people. With the $900 loaned out and $1,000 "deposited" in the bank, there is now $1,900 circulating in the economy.

Southern planters did not like this practice, because they thought it unfairly favored people who benefited from bank loans. These included northern manufacturers who needed bank loans to finance their operation.

Europe. In order to do that, the national government would have to drive innovation and encourage investment. Hamilton's plan had endorsement from President Washington, who saw the good that would come from "new and useful inventions from abroad" as well as "the exertions and skill and genius in producing them at home." To the federalists, peace, prosperity, and stability would be achieved through a unified central government that would rival those of Europe.

Jefferson and the Rise of the Democratic-Republicans

Not everyone was on board with Hamilton's plan. On the one hand, opinion was split among the states over the topic of consolidation of state debt in the federal government. These debts were distributed disproportionately. Massachusetts, Connecticut, and South Carolina owed nearly half of the sum of state-held debt. Meanwhile, Virginia, Maryland, and Georgia had already paid off large parts of their debts, and they were hardly willing to assume more taxes in order to finance other states' debts.

To people like Thomas Jefferson and his colleague James Madison, a representative from Virginia, Hamilton's proposal ran counter to everything Americans had fought for in the revolution. Jefferson imagined that Hamilton's proposal would lead the United States to look just like Great Britain, which a century ago had itself gone through a similar dramatic restructuring of national debt. Just as Great Britain had done with London-based merchants, Hamilton's proposal would consolidate power in the more cosmopolitan North at the expense of southerners. Once power had collected with a few wealthy northern merchants and manufacturers, the United States would be left with exactly the same situation it had been in under Great Britain: a small monied class lording its privilege over agrarian commoners. As the Virginia legislature had written in December 1790, Hamilton's plan not only "perpetuated upon the nation an enormous debt" but also granted the executive "unbounded influence, which … bears down all opposition and daily threatens everything

"A Peep into the Antifederal Club" (1793) depicts Jefferson standing on top of a table and giving a speech to a mob of, in the artist's view, unsavory characters.

that appertains to English liberty." Fearing that the United States would soon become the very thing they declared independence from, they wrote, "The same causes produce the same effects."

President George Washington acted against the advice of his home state of Virginia and his secretary of state, Jefferson, and signed Hamilton's plan into law on February 25, 1791. However, opposition to the Federalist program continued to gain momentum. This movement started to revolve around Jefferson, already well known as the architect of the Declaration of Independence and a stalwart defender of the rights of man, whose utopian ideals of an agrarian society of reasonable citizens acting under limited government attracted the likes of James Madison.

Jefferson assumed the role of Democratic-Republican leader reluctantly. From his vantage point as secretary of state, Jefferson witnessed the march to centralization at the hands of what he called "monarchical federalists." Among them was John Adams, with whom Jefferson had worked closely on the matter of independence. Adams had previously been called a monarchist when he motioned to introduce formal titles in the Senate. In 1790, Adams tried to justify his beliefs with "Discourses on Davila," a paper that made the case for the necessity of titles, distinctions, and rank in all forms governments, even in democratic republics. Jefferson privately commented on Adams' paper, saying that "something is at length to be publickly said against the political heresies which have sprung up among us." Jefferson was embarrassed to learn, however, that his quote was circulated in newspapers up and down the nation.

Hamilton and the other federalists, in turn, started to believe that Jefferson was organizing opposition to the government. Hamilton began a prolific writing campaign to address concerns about national centralization, accusing Jefferson of being a political malcontent bent on destroying the Constitution, national unity, and all the benefits that had come from it.

In May 1792, Jefferson wrote to Washington about his fears that Hamilton and the other members of the "corrupt squadron" were "prepar[ing] the way for a change from the present republican form of government to that of a monarchy, of which the English constitution is to be the model." Although Washington tried to assure Jefferson that there was no plot to institute a monarchy, Jefferson was unconvinced. Washington quickly found his cabinet meetings, which included the secretaries of state and treasury, Jefferson and Hamilton, devolving into an ideological brawl. In August 1792, Washington had to write his secretaries to act with "more charity for the opinions and acts of one another."

By this point, the ideological cornerstone of the Republican party had already been cast: small government was the rallying cry of many politicians and common Americans who feared the direction

America was taking. However, Republicans, especially Jefferson, recoiled from becoming an organized party. Parties originate among likeminded people to mobilize support for party politicians in order to institutionalize their political beliefs. However, Jefferson believed that parties that formed "merely by a greediness for office, as in England" were "unworthy of a reasonable or moral man." However, starting in 1793, **partisanship** within the national legislature had started to emerge as certain representatives started voting consistently in line with either Federalist or Republican ideologies. Whether he wanted it or not, Jefferson had inspired an opposition party in the United States, one based on his vision of learned ruralists crusading for individual liberty, which was threatened by the ever expanding maw of centralized government.

The Race to the Presidency

Republican ideals gained traction among the American people toward the end of Washington's presidency. When Washington left office in 1796, it set off the first contested presidential election in the United States, this one fought between the Federalists and their nominee John Adams, and the Democratic-Republicans supporting Thomas Jefferson. The Democratic-Republicans launched into a campaign based on **mud slinging** to elect Jefferson, publishing literature that said, "Thomas Jefferson is a firm REPUBLICAN—John Adams is an avowed MONARCHIST." Jefferson lost the election to Adams by only three electoral votes, becoming Adams' vice president.

Four years later, at the end of Adams' term, Jefferson and Adams went head to head again. This election was even dirtier than the previous one. The federalists had alleged during the campaign that Jefferson was an **atheist**. On July 3, 1800, the Baltimore American published rumors that Jefferson had died at Monticello, presumably in an attempt to secure the election for Adams (after all, one can't vote for a dead man). Although the rumor was circulated by several other newspapers, the truth was made known three days later. The article did little to halt the Democratic-Republicans' momentum, however, gaining ground in the traditionally federalist strongholds of New York and Pennsylvania, thanks in part to a populist from New York named Aaron Burr, who ran alongside Jefferson and undermined Adams' influence in the North.

In autumn of 1800, Jefferson won the popular vote, but there was question if the Electoral College, which actually elects the president, would ignore the will of the American people and cast their votes in favor of Burr. As the electoral votes came in, Jefferson and Burr were tied. The vote was sent to the House of Representatives, who would decide who would be president and who would be vice president. While Alexander Hamilton did not like Jefferson, he disliked Burr more. Hamilton campaigned among the representatives to vote in favor of Jefferson. (When Burr heard of Hamilton's dealings, he challenged him to a duel in 1804, which proved fatal to Hamilton). On February 17, 1781, Thomas Jefferson became the third president of the United States.

Jefferson's Record as President

Jefferson's presidency was largely characterized by the struggle to reconcile Democratic-Republican ideals of limited government with the power of his office. "I feel a great load of public favor and public expectation," Jefferson wrote after his inauguration. "More confidence is placed in me that my qualifications merit, and I dread the disappointment of my friends."

Jefferson did endeavor to limit the federal government, which had grown significantly during the terms of Washington and Adams. He cut taxes and national spending. He reduced the national debt from $83 million to $57 million, slashing the nation's obligations by nearly a third. Jefferson also downsized the military to prerevolutionary levels and reduced the navy to a handful of ships.

However, the executive office of president, with its broad powers to enforce law and enter into treaties with foreign governments, largely stood in opposition to Jefferson's ideals. While Jefferson did go a long way toward scaling back the Hamiltonian federalism that had crept its way into the national government, Jefferson wasn't above wielding his power in ways he thought would benefit the country at large.

Jefferson's presidency marked two crucial events that went a long way toward establishing the precedent of federal interventionism. The first of these happened in 1803, when Jefferson purchased the Louisiana Territory from the French emperor Napoleon. The **Louisiana Purchase** contained most of the land in the modern-day continental United States west of the Mississippi River, stretching as far north as Saskatchewan, Canada, and as far south as New Orleans, Louisiana. While the transfer amounted to the largest territorial gain in the United States' history—nearly doubling the size of the country at the time—the primary motivation behind the purchase was control of the Mississippi River. The Mississippi runs from Minnesota all the way to the Gulf of Mexico, which empties into the Atlantic Ocean. Control of the Mississippi would allow merchants in the western parts of the growing United States the freedom to ship their goods downriver to the port at New Orleans rather than send them east by more costly land routes to ports on the Atlantic Coast.

Although the deal was a relative bargain, with France exchanging 827,000 square miles (1.3 million square kilometers) for approximately 3 cents per acre (which figures to 42 cents today), many people, including Jefferson's opponents in the Federalist party, argued that the purchase itself did not fall within the **purview** of the federal government.

Jefferson justified the purchase on his power to negotiate and sign treaties, which is reserved for the executive branch under the Constitution. Alexander Hamilton had used a similarly loose interpretation of the Constitution when he first proposed his financial reforms, arguing that consolidating the nation's debt and

Thomas Jefferson: Architect of the Declaration of Independence

On March 10, 1804, French and American troops participated in a ceremonial transfer of power in New Orleans, Louisiana. The Louisiana Purchase doubled the size of the United States and amounted to the largest acquisition of land in US history.

Jeffersonian Philosophy in Action

establishing a national bank fell under the umbrella of "necessary and proper" powers given to the federal government.

The Embargo Act

In addition to the Louisiana Purchase, Jefferson was also faced with an international military crisis. During the **Napoleonic Wars**, Britain and France placed trade restrictions on each other in order to weaken each other economically. Up until this point, the United States had pledged to remain neutral during the conflict, supplying both sides with war material. However, both France and Britain looked to test American resolve. Britain went so far as to actively harass American vessels and capture and **press** American sailors into the Royal Navy. (By Jefferson's secretary of state James Madison's calculation, 4,028 American seamen had been captured by the British and pressed into service during the affair.) In response, Congress passed Non-Importation Acts, which restricted British manufacturers from importing goods into the United States.

The situation came to a head on June 22, 1807, when the HMS *Leopard*, which had been hunting for British naval deserters, opened fire on the USS *Chesapeake* in the waters off the Virginia coast. The Chesapeake's commanding officer, John Barron, and seventeen crew members were wounded, and three American sailors were killed. The question before the United States was whether to declare war on Great Britain. With the military reduced and most members of Congress disposed toward peace, Jefferson decided to pass the far-reaching **Embargo Act of 1807**, which prohibited American vessels from sailing in the hopes of protecting their crews from British attacks.

The act ran counter to many of the ideals of Jeffersonian republicanism and the independence of the free states, and it constituted a massive imposition into the affairs of private citizens by the federal government. America's merchant fleet could not sail, decimating American exporters. Many Americans were without jobs. Similar to the Boston Port Act imposed by Parliament before the revolution, smuggling not only grew in prevalence but also popularity, and people started to resent the government that had instituted it. Furthermore, while the embargo did manage to protect some American sailors from attack, it did little to compel Great Britain to stop attacking.

Jefferson's popularity plummeted in the wake of the passage of the Embargo Act. Jefferson received numerous letters, such as one from Bostonian Lane Jones: "How much longer are you going to keep this damned Embargo on to starve us poor people. One of my children has already starved to death of which I am ashamed and declared that it died of an apoplexy [stroke]." An anonymous letter writer wrote, "You are the damnedest fool that God put life into. God damn you." "You have brought the government to the jaws of destruction," wrote a Philadelphian under the pen name Cassandra. On March 1, 1809, just days before Jefferson would resign his office, Congress lifted the embargo and allowed America's vessels to again sail to all countries except Britain and France.

Jefferson wound down his two terms as president largely the same way he had begun them: with national controversy. This time, popular opinion had turned against him. The man who had defended his country's interest since before its inception was now forced to face the brunt of its disdain for him.

CHAPTER FIVE

Republicanism and Slavery

T homas Jefferson has been enshrined in the United States as a defender of individual liberties and a champion of the intrinsic goodness of mankind accomplished through free exercise of personal conscience. However, as much as Jefferson was devoted to the ideals of freedom and equality, there remains the issue of slavery. The same man who wrote about "self-evident" truths that "all men are created equal" and "endowed by their creator with certain unalienable rights" also owned slaves, human beings who were his property and therefore denied the benefits of liberty. This fact has led many people throughout history to wonder how—if at all—Jefferson managed to reconcile his philosophy with the institution of slavery.

Thomas Jefferson struggled his entire life to reconcile his moral and political ideals with the institution of slavery. Though he championed equality and liberty, he himself owned a large number of slaves.

Slavery in eighteenth- and nineteenth-century America was a fundamentally coercive and violent system based on the economic relationship between slave and slave owner, but Jefferson apparently tried to make his slaves' lives a little easier than most. He once wrote to Manoah Clarkson, an overseer at Monticello, in 1792, "My first wish is that the laborers may be well treated." Jefferson also apparently believed more in positive reinforcement rather than punishment, as he often tried to motivate his slaves to perform tasks in exchange for small rewards.

Nevertheless, as much as Jefferson considered himself to be an enlightened humanist, the treatment of the slaves at Monticello was deplorable. Jefferson was frequently absent from Monticello, leaving the management of his plantation to overseers like William Page, William McGehee, and Gabriel Lilly. Each man had a reputation among Jefferson's slaves for using excessive and violent corporal punishment on the slaves. Once, when the slave James Hemmings was ill, Lilly was reported to have whipped the man three times.

Jefferson's Philosophical Approach to Slavery

In his writings, Jefferson appeared to abhor the reality of slavery. As a Burgess in Virginia before the Revolutionary War, Jefferson had introduced legislation that would have outlawed the importation of new slaves. However, his bill, proposed in an assembly of Virginia planters who themselves owned hundreds of slaves, was struck down.

Jefferson again tried to undermine slavery in the colonies in his draft of the Declaration of Independence, in which he leveled an attack against King George III for initiating and institutionalizing the practice:

> He [George III] has waged cruel war against human nature itself, violating its sacred right of life and liberty in the persons of a distant people who never offended him, captivating and carrying them into slavery in another hemisphere, or to incur miserable death in

their transportation thither. This piratical warfare, the opprobrium of *infidel* powers, is the warfare of the *Christian* king of Great Britain. Determined to keep open a market where *Men* should be bought and sold, he has prostituted his negative for suppressing every legislative attempt to prohibit or to restrain this execrable commerce. And that this assemblage of horrors might want no fact of distinguished die, he is now exciting those very people to rise in arms among us, and to purchase that liberty of which he has deprived them, by murdering the people on whom he also obtruded them: thus paying off former crimes committed against the *Liberties* of one people, with crimes which he urges them to commit against the *lives* of another.

Once again, the notion was struck down, this time by delegates that spanned the colonies. The strongest opposition came from Jefferson's own colleagues as well as delegates from other slaveholding states, including Georgia, Maryland, and North and South Carolina. Those colonies in the north that did not hold slaves did not see the issue as in need of resolution at that time; the big topic of the day was independence from Great Britain, not the fate of American slaves.

Jefferson demurred to the political necessity of independence, and the paragraph was struck from the final version of the Declaration. However, Jefferson was anxious about ensuring that later generations knew of his effort, circulating several handwritten copies of his original draft as well as copying his draft in its entirety again in his autobiography. John Adams' son and the country's sixth president, John Quincy Adams, recalled Jefferson's dilemma:

He saw the gross inconsistency between the principles of the Declaration of Independence and the fact of Negro slavery, and he could not, or would not, prostitute the faculties of his mind to the vindication of slavery which from his soul he abhorred. Mr. Jefferson had not the spirit of martyrdom. He would have introduced a flaming denunciation into the Declaration of Independence, but the discretion of his colleagues struck it out.

Slavery remained a subject of debate for Jefferson. Although he had never abandoned his contention that slavery was a despicable institution and a blemish for the newfound nation of the United States, he continued to operate his plantation through the work of slaves.

In 1781, Jefferson concluded his term as governor in Virginia and retired briefly from public office. Over the next couple years, Jefferson worked on his *Notes on the State of Virginia,* a writing project he had started while governor. *Notes on the State of Virginia* is Jefferson's only full-length published work. Over the course of twenty-three chapters, *Notes on the State of Virginia* covers a variety of topics, from geography, biology, and meteorology, to history, politics, and morals. It is a broad and detailed compilation of data, discussion of good society, and a defense of Jefferson's home state.

Among the latter chapters, Jefferson also discusses the issue of slavery as experienced in Virginia. Writing for himself, Jefferson again reiterates the argument he had tried to weave into his list of grievances against Great Britain in the Declaration of Independence:

> The whole commerce between master and slave is a perpetual exercise of the most boisterous passions, the most unremitting despotism on the one part, and degrading submissions on the other. Our children see this, and learn to imitate it; for man is an imitative animal … The parent storms, the child looks on, catches the lineaments of wrath, puts on the same airs in the circle of smaller slaves, gives a loose to his worst of passions, and thus nursed, educated, and daily exercised in tyranny, cannot but be stamped by it with odious peculiarities.

SEPARATION OF FAMILIES.

By the 1800s, many Americans started to look critically at slavery and question the morality behind its practice. This cartoon points to just one of the many tragedies common to slavery.

Slavery to Jefferson was a particularly dangerous institution in the newly free United States. Not only was it depraved in and of itself, but it also weakened the moral fiber of those involved in its continuation. Because of democratic-republicanism's understanding that democracy hinges on men's education and their ability to morally reason, the fact that slavery harmed not only slaves but also free men's consciences and threatened the survival of the new nation itself.

Despite Jefferson's repeated calls for an end to slavery in Virginia and in the United States as a whole, he nevertheless maintained opinions of black Americans that can only be described as racist.

I advance it therefore as a suspicion only, that the blacks, whether originally a distinct race, or made distinct by time and circumstances, are inferior to the whites in the endowments both of body and mind ... This unfortunate difference of color, and perhaps of faculty, is a powerful obstacle to the emancipation of these people. Many of their advocates, while they wish to vindicate the liberty of human nature, are anxious also to preserve its dignity and beauty. Some of these, embarrassed by the question 'What further is to be done with them?' join themselves in opposition with those who are actuated by sordid avarice only. Among the Romans emancipation required but one effort. The slave, when made free, might mix with, without staining the blood of his master. But with us a second is necessary, unknown to history. When freed, he is to be removed beyond the reach of mixture.

As abominable as the institution of slavery was to Jefferson, he saw black people themselves as inherently inferior to whites. Comparing slavery in America to ancient Roman slavery, which Jefferson thinks was an instance of whites enslaving whites, Jefferson raises the issue of interracial relationships. Because of the supposed innate superiority of whites, Jefferson remarks that such intermingling must be avoided. To Jefferson, the necessity of emancipation is counterbalanced by the practical difficulty of removing blacks from the American population.

A Lifelong Question

Jefferson grappled with the issue of slavery for his entire life. In his correspondence and personal writings, during his political career as well as in his retirement, Jefferson continued to question both the practice of enslavement as well as the character of enslaved people.

RUN away from the subscriber in *Albemarle*, a Mulatto slave called *Sandy*, about 35 years of age, his stature is rather low, inclining to corpulence, and his complexion light; he is a shoemaker by trade, in which he uses his left hand principally, can do coarse carpenters work, and is something of a horse jockey; he is greatly addicted to drink, and when drunk is insolent and disorderly, in his conversation he swears much, and in his behaviour is artful and knavish. He took with him a white horse, much scarred with traces, of which it is expected he will endeavour to dispose; he also carried his shoemakers tools, and will probably endeavour to get employment that way. Whoever conveys the said slave to me, in *Albemarle*, shall have 40 s. reward, if taken up within the county, 4 l. if elsewhere within the colony, and 10 l. if in any other colony, from

THOMAS JEFFERSON.

In September 1769, Jefferson placed the above ad in the *Virginia Gazette* offering a reward in exchange for the return of a runaway slave.

During his time in France, Jefferson had become familiar with Nicholas de Condorcet, a French philosopher who wrote extensively on slavery. When Jefferson returned to the United States, he wrote Condorcet of a black mathematician who had been hired to design the country's new capitol. Jefferson spoke highly of the man, and considered him to be a productive member in free society. However, the mathematician was to Jefferson an exception rather than the rule. Jefferson wrote that he would "be delighted to see these instances of moral eminence so multiplied as to prove that the want of talents observed in them is merely the effect of their degraded condition, and not proceeding from any difference in the structure of the parts in which intellect demands." The irony of Jefferson refusing to acknowledge the worth of a black man employed in designing the capitol of the United

SALLY HEMINGS

Before she died on September 6, 1782, Patty Jefferson made her husband promise that he would not remarry and subject their children to living under a stepmother. Jefferson honored this promise for this whole life. However, since his time in Williamsburg, Jefferson was fired with a passion for women that would not wane. Jefferson had dalliances with women after his wife's passing, but none have reached the level of recognition as his relationship with a slave woman named Sarah "Sally" Hemings.

The Hemings family were part of Jefferson's inheritance when Patty's father, John Wayles, died in 1774. Sally was born to Elizabeth Hemings and John Wayles, according to her son Madison (who wrote the greatest amount of firsthand information about Hemings' relationship with Jefferson), which made her both mixed-race and Patty Jefferson's half-sister. In 1787, while Jefferson was traveling in France, he requested that his daughter, eight-year-old Mary, join him. Sally, fourteen at the time, accompanied the girl as her maid. At some point during their journey through France, Jefferson entered into a sexual relationship with Sally. (It was not unusual for white slave owners to take their slaves as concubines, which often constituted rape because the women did so against their own will.)

In a surprising turn, when Jefferson made plans to return to Virginia, Sally, now pregnant, refused to go. At that time, France had a rule that allowed enslaved persons to apply for freedom with or without the approval of their masters. In France, Sally was free; returning to Virginia would mean a return to the status quo. Jefferson, who had always enjoyed a level of control as an aristocrat from Virginia, was now forced to negotiate with his slave. In order to convince Sally to return with him, he promised her preferential treatment at home and pledged to free her children when they reached the age of twenty-one. Shortly after returning to Virginia, Sally had her first child. Over the years, she would give birth to six children, four of whom survived.

On September 1, 1802, the Jefferson-Hemings affair became the talk of the town when James Callender reported in the *Richmond Reporter*, "It is well known that the man, *whom it delighteth the people to honor*, keeps, and for many years has kept, as his concubine, one of his own slaves. Her name is Sally ... By this wench Sally, our president has had several children." The scandal was

A PHILOSOPHIC COCK

When word got out that Jefferson had had an affair and fathered children with his slave Sally Hemings, many newspapers took the opportunity to embarrass and ridicule the president.

widely circulated throughout the country, but Jefferson never acknowledged his participation in the affair or the question of the children's paternity during his lifetime. However, in 1998, a DNA study of Sally's male descendants showed that their genes matched those of Jefferson's known male descendants. Today, most historians, including the Thomas Jefferson Foundation, believe that Jefferson fathered six children with Sally Hemings.

States—in helping to build the political axis of a free nation through his own efforts—should not be lost on modern audiences.

Whatever Jefferson felt about black people's intrinsic worth and intellectual capacities, he believed that these issues could not and should not translate to government policy. The relative worth of one person over another did not factor into Republican ideology. Jefferson put it thus: "Whatever be their [blacks'] degree of talent it is no measure of their rights. Because Sir Isaac Newton was superior to others in understanding, he was not therefore lord of the person or property of others." Rather than allow the United States to be subject to a meritocracy in which power is shared only among those deemed most worthy of it, the American experiment and its benefits of freedom and equality ought to be distributed to all people.

As Jefferson approached the end of his life, he began to worry about the fate of his nation. He wrote in his autobiography about the path America was on and the cosmic justice that would soon be exacted upon it:

> Indeed I tremble for my country when I reflect that God is just: that his justice cannot sleep for ever: that considering numbers, nature and natural means only, a revolution of the wheel of fortune, an exchange of situation, is among possible events: that it may become probable by supernatural interference! The Almighty has no attribute which can take sides with us in such a contest.

As slavery continued to be further entrenched in the first decades of the United States, Jefferson feared that a reckoning would be due. Later in his *Autobiography*, Jefferson refers to black Americans as "our suffering brethren."

In the end, the economic expedience of owning slaves outweighed Jefferson's decades of philosophical wrangling on the issue. Like many Virginia slaveholders of his time, the bottom line for slavery came down to dollars and cents. Jefferson had struggled for most of his life to remain financially solvent, inheriting both his father's and his father-in-law's debts when they passed. Operating a large plantation with slaves helped Jefferson stay afloat.

As repugnant as the institution was, as necessary as the emancipation of slaves was, Jefferson could not bring himself to realize his own vision. When Jefferson died, he freed only a handful of his slaves. Although Jefferson's situation was not unique among American planters, and **abolitionism** as a movement would not reach wide appeal in the United States until many decades after Jefferson, there were still several slaveholders who granted freedom to their servants and slaves when they died, such as George Washington, also a Virginian. While it is easy to defend Jefferson as simply a product of his culture's heritage, he was never a conventional Virginia planter. Few other slaveholders studied moral and political philosophy as deeply as Jefferson. Certainly none of them had breathed life into a nation with the words "all men are created equal."

It is possible that there may never be a complete understanding of Jefferson's attitude about slaves and slavery. That the Founding Father who articulated the ideals of equality and liberty so eloquently also so conclusively denied them to people within his own household remains a stain on the United States' history.

CHAPTER SIX

Jefferson's America

fter leaving Washington largely in disgrace, Jefferson spent the last seventeen years of his life on his estate in Monticello. During this time, Jefferson embarked on more philanthropic pursuits, most of which focused on expanding education. He sold his vast library to the government, which would form the foundation for the Library of Congress. In 1818, Jefferson got to realize his vision of a publicly-funded center for education when the Virginia Legislature approved a state university, the University of Virginia.

Adams and Jefferson: Best of Frenemies

In the wake of his presidency, Jefferson endeavored to repair his relationship with John Adams. The two had worked together

This portrait of Thomas Jefferson was painted by Thomas Sully in 1822, just four years before Jefferson's death.

closely to draft the declaration but, during Adams' presidency, their conflicting ideologies about the role and extent of government led to animosity between them.

After the revolution, Adams started to suffer from jealousy. Although he had proved instrumental in jumpstarting the independence movement, he was never first in line for credit. Although Adams had been a proponent of revolution from the beginning, he understood the importance of sacrificing personal battles in order to win larger wars—a lesson he followed begrudgingly. Adams represented the most aggrieved colony in the budding union, Massachusetts, which should have given him a certain moral authority on the subject of independence. However, he was forced to lead from behind by slowly revealing to his colleagues the actuality of war and the necessity of independence.

Part of that strategy also meant passing up the opportunity to draft the Declaration of Independence, a task that he largely handed to Thomas Jefferson. While Jefferson crafted the document, Adams had a hand in editing it. Of course, Jefferson received the bulk of credit for having written it in the first place. In fact, it often seems more people recognize Ben Franklin's contribution as an editor for the words "self evident" than Adams's. It may have been because of his largely behind-the-scenes work that Adams ultimately lost the new nation's first presidential election to George Washington, whose achievements on the battlefield were much more apparent than Adams's subtle political maneuvering and personal sacrifices.

Jefferson became the object of Adams's dissatisfaction. Adams wrote to his son, John Quincy Adams, in a letter dated January 3, 1794:

> Ambition is the subtlest Beast of the Intellectual and Moral Field. It is wonderfully adroit in concealing itself from its owner ... Jefferson thinks he shall by this step get a Reputation of a humble, modest, meek man, wholly without ambition or vanity. He may even have deceived himself of this Belief. But if a Prospect opens, the World

will see and he will see, that he is as ambitious as Oliver Cromwell though no soldier.

When Adams was elected president in 1797, he would again be forced to work with his now political nemesis, Thomas Jefferson. Because of a provision in the Constitution at the time, the second-highest vote earner in a presidential election secured the office of vice president. Jefferson had lost to Adams by only three electoral votes. This differs from the modern American electoral process, where president and vice president, who are usually from the same party, run on the same ticket. The reason for this change in American elections was the same reason for Adams's feelings of exasperation during his presidency.

Given these opposing political views, Adams and Jefferson sparred on nearly every issue. More often than not, Jefferson stood in the way of many of Adams's wishes, making for a fraught presidency characterized by constant **gridlock**. Adams wrote to his wife Abigail, "My country has in its wisdom contrived for me the most insignificant office that ever the invention of man contrived or his imagination conceived … I can do neither good nor evil."

Years after Adams's presidency, Jefferson wished in an 1813 letter to Adams that "[y]ou and I ought not to die, before we have explained ourselves to each other." Jefferson and Adams remained close friends through the rest of their lives, exchanging a huge body of correspondence up to their deaths.

Jefferson's Final Months

Jefferson's health was failing as the fiftieth anniversary of the signing of the Declaration of Independence in 1826 approached. In Washington, those organizing the celebration in the nation's capital requested that he return to the city to join in the festivities, but Jefferson was already homebound by that point. Instead, he wrote to commemorate the occasion:

All eyes are opened, or opening, to the rights of man. The general spread of the light of science has already laid open to every new view the palpable truth that the mass of mankind has not been born with saddles on their backs, nor a few favored booted and spurred, ready to ride them legitimately, by the grace of God. These are grounds of hope for others. For ourselves, let the annual return of this day forever refresh our recollections of these rights, and an undiminished devotion to them.

These would be the last words he would give to the nation he had breathed life into.

On June 24, 1826, Jefferson wrote to Dr. Robley Dunglinson to come to Monticello to attend to his failing health. Jefferson, now eighty-three, was approaching the end of his life. Over the next several days, Jefferson slipped in and out of consciousness. Dunglinson and others remained at his bedside, giving him medicine until July 3, when Jefferson waved it away saying, "No, Doctor, nothing more."

Throughout the day, Jefferson lay in anticipation of the Fourth of July, the anniversary of the birth of his nation, asking those gathered around him if the day had come. Moments before midnight, Jefferson woke, and asked Nicholas Trist if it was the fourth yet. Trist lied and said it was, hoping not to disappoint Jefferson. "Ah," Jefferson said: "Just as I wished." Perhaps detecting it was not yet time, Jefferson held out a few hours more. He at last received his wish, passing in his bed at his beloved Monticello just before one o'clock that July afternoon.

Jefferson's Legacy

The United States has come a long way since the turn of the eighteenth century. What was once a sparse collection of British descendants residing on the east coast of America in thirteen backwoods colonies is now among the most powerful nations on earth, encompassing fifty states stretching across the entire continent, and populated by people of varying religions, backgrounds, occupations, and nationalities. However, the United States is—as it perhaps always has been—a study in contradiction. On the one hand, the debate about the balance of power between the states and the federal government rages on, although federal powers have expanded considerably in the nearly three decades since the United States' founding. More people can vote than in the eighteenth century, with a rapidly expanding population and women and minorities granted the right to vote; yet political power has been largely divested from people, as corporations with vastly greater wealth and access to politicians have been recently granted personhood by the Supreme Court. The diversity of religions in America is at an all-time high; yet many business people and politicians advance agendas that in many ways resemble the sort of institutionalized religion that was characteristic of monarchy.

Despite these modern problems of government, however, American society continues to be Jeffersonian. The ideals that Jefferson had imbued the United States with nearly three centuries ago continue to speak to us. Jefferson himself—who occupied the public arena, yet was constantly pulled toward matters of home; who championed the common man, yet was himself a product of aristocracy and privilege; who fought for political equality and liberty, yet owned slaves—was a contradiction, as much as modern American society is today. In Jefferson lies the hope of a nation. Jefferson said, and in many ways demonstrated himself, that through uncertainty and hardship, despite the prejudices and fears of people, there remains an incorruptible dignity in the human spirit; and it is with this spirit that real change is possible. This philosophy has been immortalized in America's founding document, the Declaration of Independence. Though worn and fading, its principles continue to shape our world. As Jefferson's friend John Adams said:

> It stands, and must forever stand, alone, a beacon on the summit of the mountain, to which all the inhabitants of

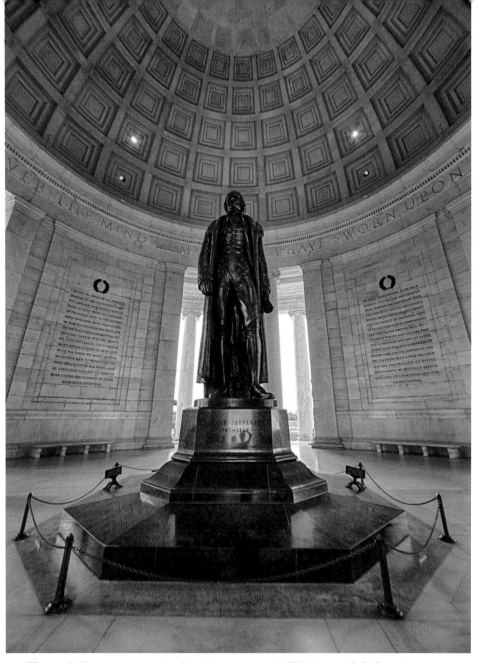

Thomas Jefferson is memorialized in this monument in Washington, DC. Carved into the walls around the central statue are excerpts from Jefferson's writings, including *A Summary View*, the bill establishing religious freedom in Virginia, and, of course, the Declaration of Independence.

the earth may turn their eyes for a genial and saving light till time shall be lost in eternity, and this globe itself dissolve, nor leave a wreck behind. It stands for ever, a light of admonition to the rulers of men, a light of salvation and redemption to the oppressed... [as the delineation of] the boundaries of their respective rights and duties, founded in the laws of nature, and of nature's God.

The United States has never been perfect, and it likely never will be. The liberty that brings out the best in American society is also the vehicle for realizing its worst. However, in the darkest moments, Jefferson's words remain, shining brightly from the summit of the mountain.

Both Jefferson and Adams died on the same day, July 4, 1826, with Jefferson passing just hours before Adams. In his final moments, Adams' thoughts turned to his friend, Jefferson. With his final breath, Adams spoke, "Thomas Jefferson survives."

And he does.

CHRONOLOGY

1743 On April 13, Thomas Jefferson is born at Shadwell, Virginia, to Peter and Jane Randolph Jefferson.

1757 Peter Jefferson dies on August 17.

1760–1762 Thomas Jefferson studies at the College of William and Mary in Williamsburg, Virginia.

1762 Jefferson is introduced to the renowned attorney George Wythe, under whom he studies law.

1763 Great Britain and France cease conflict in the Seven Years' War (also known as the French and Indian War in the British North American colonies); Britain wins but is left with staggering debt as a result.

1764 Jefferson turns twenty-one, thereby inheriting his father's estate.

1765 Parliament passes the Stamp Act, levying a tax on several kinds of printed materials and official documents on the colonies to raise revenue; protests against British taxation begin in the colonies.

1767 Parliament passes the Townshend Act, taxing things such as paint, glass, paper, and tea.

1768 Jefferson is elected to the Virginia House of Burgesses.

1770 On February 1, a fire at Shadwell destroys Jefferson's childhood home. Jefferson moves to Monticello.

1770 On March 5, British redcoats open fire into a crowd of protestors, who had been violently harassing a sentinel in front of the Boston Customs House. A total of five Americans die, prompting colonial newspapers to call the event the "Boston Massacre."

1772 On January 1, Jefferson marries widow Martha Wayles Skelton; their first daughter, Martha, is born later that year.

1773 On May 10, Parliament passes the Tea Act, giving preferential treatment to the struggling British East India Company and establishing stricter law enforcement protocols for smugglers. On May 16, Jefferson's friend Dabney Carr dies.

1773 On December 16, the Boston-based patriot group the Sons of Liberty, under the direction of Samuel Adams, dumps British tea worth ten thousand pounds into the harbor, an event that becomes known as the Boston Tea Party.

1774 Parliament passes the Intolerable Acts (also known as the Coercive Acts) intended to beat the colonies into submission. Boston's port is closed, restricting the city's commerce and sending thousands of residents into unemployment. The colonies call for the first Continental Congress to discuss the official colonial reaction to Britain's encroachment. Jefferson writes *A Summary View of the Rights of British America*, to be delivered to the Congress. He inherits 11,000 acres of land and 135 slaves from John Wayles, his father-in-law (Jefferson keeps the slaves but sells most of the land to settle debts).

1775 On April 19 and 20, British troops clash with colonial militia at Lexington and Concord, Massachusetts.

1775–1776 Jefferson attends the Second Continental Congress in Philadelphia, Pennsylvania.

1776 In June, Jefferson drafts the Declaration of Independence.

1776 On July 4, the Continental Congress ratifies the Declaration of Independence, making the united colonies an independent nation.

1779 Jefferson introduces the State for Religious Freedom in the Virginia legislature.

1779–1781 Jefferson serves as Virginia's governor.

1780 Jefferson begins writing *Notes on the State of Virginia*.

1782 Martha Wayles Jefferson dies.

1784–1789 Jefferson lives in France acting as Commissioner and Minister; begins a relationship with one of his slaves, Sally Hemings.

1787 Jefferson publishes *Notes on the State of Virginia*.

1788 The new United States Constitution is ratified by New Hampshire, the last state to agree to it; the Constitution balances the power between the states and the federal government by creating an executive branch capable of enforcing laws passed by the national legislature and a judiciary to supervise it.

1790–1793 President George Washington selects Thomas Jefferson to be the first US secretary of state.

1797–1801 Jefferson becomes US vice president under John Adams, losing to him by only three electoral votes.

1801 On February 17, Jefferson is elected president of the United States by the House of Representatives, beating Aaron Burr.

1803 The US government purchases the Louisiana Territory from France for fifteen million dollars, doubling the size of the nation.

1807 On June 22, the British naval ship HMS *Leopard* opens fire on the USS *Chesapeake* off the coast of Virginia when the *Chesapeake* refuses to allow British sailors aboard to search for deserters. The US government begins to consider the possibility of war with Britain.

1807 On December 22, President Jefferson signs the Embargo Act of 1807, closing off American ports and prohibiting American ships from sailing.

1809 The Embargo Act is repealed by Congress; days later, Jefferson resigns from office largely in public disgrace.

1815 Jefferson sells his library to Congress, numbering 6,700 books, providing the seed for what would become the Library of Congress.

1825 The University of Virginia opens.

1826 Jefferson dies at Monticello on July 4, exactly fifty years after the signing of the Declaration of Independence.

GLOSSARY

abolitionism The movement toward ending slavery.

Articles of Confederation The organizing law of the United States prior to the passage of the Constitution; characterized by a weak central government consisting of a single legislative body with no powers to enforce its laws.

atheist A person who believes that there is no God.

Bill of Rights The name for the first ten amendments to the Constitution, ratified in 1791, that guarantee certain rights to the states and individual citizens, such as the right to free religion, free speech, free assembly, etc.

colony An area that is under full or partial control by another country, typically a distant one, and inhabited primarily by settlers from the country.

Constitution (US) The law organizing the United States' government, which includes a bicameral (two-house) legislature (Congress), an executive (the president), and a judiciary (the Supreme Court); replaced the Articles of Confederation.

Continental Congress The name for the assembly of elected delegates from each of the thirteen British colonies leading up to the Revolutionary War.

creditor Someone who loans money.

Crown A term that refers to the British government, especially the monarchy.

debtor Someone who owes money.

Democratic-Republicans A political party based on Jeffersonian ideals of limited government that rose up in response to Federalism.

disenfranchise To deprive someone or a group of people of rights, privileges, and/or political powers that they are owed.

effigy A rough model of a person made to be destroyed in protest; leading up to the revolution, effigies of well-known loyalists were paraded, slashed, hanged, burned, and beheaded during patriot protests.

embargo An official ban on trade with one or more countries.

Embargo Act of 1807 A law passed by Congress and signed by Jefferson in response to British military action off the coast of the United States that closed American ports and prohibited American vessels from sailing.

Enlightenment A philosophical movement in the seventeenth and eighteenth centuries and centered primarily in Western Europe that emphasized knowledge through individual human reason instead of relying on long-held tradition.

federal government The national government of the United States.

Federalists A political party that advocated for a strong centralized government, especially one envisioned by Alexander Hamilton that controlled all national debts and operated a central bank.

gridlock The term for political standstill brought about by two competing ideologies or parties in government working against one another.

humanism An Enlightenment principle that gave importance to human experience over superstition, tradition, and religion; emphasized intrinsic worth of humans and the necessity to act rationally.

legislature The branch of government tasked with creating new laws.

liberal Someone or something that follows Enlightenment philosophy, which took a favorable view of humanity, and therefore champions individual rights and liberties.

Louisiana Purchase The transfer of the Louisiana Territory, which included most of the lands in the continental United States west of the Mississippi River, from France to the United States.

loyalist A supporter of the British government before and during the American Revolution.

martial law When the highest-ranking military officer becomes head of government during times of political crisis.

migraine A debilitating headache characterized by nausea and sensitivity to light.

Monticello The name for Jefferson's estate located in Albemarle County in Virginia.

mud slinging The practice of one politician trying to defame another during a political campaign.

Napoleonic Wars A series of wars between France and Great Britain as a result of Napoleon Bonaparte's drive to create a French empire in Europe following the French Revolution.

neoclassical An architectural movement that drew inspiration from ancient Greek and Roman (i.e. "classical") architecture; characterized by such elements as ornate columns, visual symmetry, and domed roofs.

partisanship Prejudice arising from two political parties with differing views on the goals and extent of government.

press (also impress) To force someone into something, especially military service, without their consent.

primogeniture The practice of giving a family's firstborn descendant, especially a son, the entirety of a person's property on their death; primogeniture was prevalent in the Middle Ages as a means to keep property, wealth, and power intact within one family throughout generations.

purview The scope of influence or control over something.

ratify To sign or otherwise agree to something, making it official valid.

resolution A formal expression of intent by a legislative body, such as the Declaration of Independence.

revolution The forcible overthrow of a government in favor of a new one.

sacrosanct Holy; too important to be altered.

stoic A person who can endure pain or other hardship while maintaining a calm outward appearance.

treason The crime of undermining one's country, such as by attempting to overthrow the established government.

treaty A formal agreement between two countries, such as the one concluding the Louisiana Purchase.

SOURCES

⌒

INTRODUCTION

pg. 6: Melton, Buckner F. Jr. *The Quotable Founding Fathers: A Treasury of 2,500 Wise and Witty Quotations From the Men and Women Who Created America* (Dulles, Virginia: Potomac Books, 2004), p. 55.

pg. 6: Heathcote, William. "Franklin's Contributions to the American Revolution as a Diplomat in France," www.ushistory. org/valleyforge/history/franklin.html.

CHAPTER 1

pg. 10: Meacham, Jon. *Thomas Jefferson: The Art of Power* (New York: Random House, 2013), p. 5.

pg. 12: *Ibid.*, p. 8.

pg. 12: Kennedy, John F. "Remarks at a Dinner Honoring Nobel Prize Winners of the Western Hemisphere," http://www. presidency.ucsb.edu/ws/?pid=8623.

pg. 13: "Shadwell," www.monticello.org/site/research-and-collections/shadwell.

pg. 13: Meacham, Jon. *Thomas Jefferson: The Art of Power* (New York: Random House, 2013), p. 46.

pg. 14: Jefferson, Thomas. "From Thomas Jefferson to John Page 15 July 1763," founders.archives.gov/documents/Jefferson/01-01-02-0004.

pg. 14: Jefferson, Thomas. "Thomas Jefferson to Dabney Carr, 19 January 1816"." founders.archives.gov/documents/ Jefferson/03-09-02-0238.

pg.16: Jefferson, Thomas. "Extract from Thomas Jefferson to George R. Gilmer," http://tjrs.monticello.org/letter/96.

pg. 18: Jefferson, Thomas. "Hunting." www.monticello.org/site /research-and-collections/hunting.

pg. 19: Meacham, Jon. *Thomas Jefferson: The Art of Power* (New York: Random House, 2013), p. 19.

pg. 19: "Exercise," www.monticello.org/site/research-and- collections/exercise.

pg. 20: Meacham, Jon. *Thomas Jefferson: The Art of Power* (New York: Random House, 2013), p. 25.

pg. 20: *Ibid.*, p. 17.

pg. 20: *Ibid.*, p. 18.

pg. 22: Kant, Immanuel. "What is the Enlightenment?" http:// www.columbia.edu/acis/ets/CCREAD/etscc/kant.html.

pg. 23: Meacham, Jon. *Thomas Jefferson: The Art of Power* (New York: Random House, 2013), p. 22.

CHAPTER 2

pg. 29: Nash, Gary B. *The Unknown American Revolution: The Unruly Birth of Democracy and the Struggle to Create America.* (New York: Penguin Group, 2005), p. 178.

pg. 29: *Ibid.*, p. 180.

pg. 39: Meacham, Jon. *Thomas Jefferson: The Art of Power* (New York: Random House, 2013), p. 71

pg. 41: Young, Ralph F. *Dissent in America: 400 Years of Speeches, Sermons, Arguments, Articles, Letters, and Songs That Made a Difference.* (New York: Pearson Education, Inc., 2008), p. 65.

CHAPTER 3

pg. 44: Meacham, Jon. *Thomas Jefferson: The Art of Power* (New York: Random House, 2013), p. 123.

pg. 44: "Thomas Jefferson and the Virginia Stature for Religious Freedom," www.vahistorical.org/collections-and-resources/virginia-history-explorer/Thomas-Jefferson.

pg. 45: Wood, Gordon S. *Empire of Liberty: A History of the Early Republic, 1789–1815.* (New York: Oxford University Press, 2009), p. 101.

pg. 47: Meacham, Jon. *Thomas Jefferson: The Art of Power* (New York: Random House, 2013), p. 75.

pg. 47: *Ibid.*

pg. 48: Meacham, Jon. *Thomas Jefferson: The Art of Power* (New York: Random House, 2013), p. 79.

pg. 50: *Ibid.*, p. 81.

pg. 51: *Ibid.*, p. 88.

pg. 51: *Ibid.*, p. 87.

pg. 53: *Ibid.*, p. 100.

pg. 55: *Ibid.*, p. 102.

pg. 55: *Ibid.*

pg. 55: Meacham, Jon. *Thomas Jefferson: The Art of Power* (New York: Random House, 2013), p. 22.

pg. 56: *Ibid.*, p. 103.

pg. 59: Young, Ralph F. *Dissent in America: 400 Years of Speeches, Sermons, Arguments, Articles, Letters, and Songs That Made a Difference.* (New York: Pearson Education, Inc., 2008), pp. 58–59.

pg. 59: *Ibid.*, p. 65.

pg. 60: *Ibid.*, 2013), p. 106.

pg. 60: *Ibid.*

pg. 62: Melton, Buckner F. Jr. *The Quotable Founding Fathers: A Treasury of 2,500 Wise and Witty Quotations From the Men and Women Who Created America* (Dulles, Virginia: Potomac Books, 2004), p. 55.

pg. 62: McCullough, David. *1776.* (New York: Simon & Schuster, 2006), p. 137.

pg. 63: *Ibid.*

pg. 63: *Ibid.*, p. 136.

CHAPTER 4

pg. 68: Meacham, Jon. *Thomas Jefferson: The Art of Power* (New York: Random House, 2013), p. 123.

pp. 68: "Thomas Jefferson and the Virginia Stature for Religious Freedom," www.vahistorical.org/collections-and-resources/virginia-history-explorer/Thomas-Jefferson.

pg. 74: Wood, Gordon S. *Empire of Liberty: A History of the Early Republic, 1789–1815*. (New York: Oxford University Press, 2009), p. 101.

pg. 75: *Ibid.*, p. 145.

pg. 75: *Ibid.*

pg. 76: Wood, Gordon S. *Empire of Liberty: A History of the Early Republic, 1789–1815*. (New York: Oxford University Press, 2009), p. 146.

pg. 76: *Ibid.*, p. 154.

pg. 76: *Ibid.*, p. 155.

pg. 77: *Ibid.*, p. 162.

pg. 78: Meacham, Jon. *Thomas Jefferson: The Art of Power* (New York: Random House, 2013), p. 351.

pg. 83: *Ibid.*, p. 433.

pg. 83: *Ibid.*

CHAPTER 5

pg. 86: "Property." www.monticello.org/site/plantation-and-slavery/property.

pg. 87: Melton, Buckner F. Jr. *The Quotable Founding Fathers: A Treasury of 2,500 Wise and Witty Quotations From the Men and Women Who Created America* (Dulles, Virginia: Potomac Books, 2004), p. 293.

pg. 88: *Ibid.*, p. 146.

pg. 88: Meacham, Jon. *Thomas Jefferson: The Art of Power* (New York: Random House, 2013), p. 10.

pg. 90: Jefferson, Thomas. *Notes on the State of Virginia,* docsouth. unc.edu/southlit/jefferson/jefferson.html.

pg. 91: Matthews, Richard K. *The Radical Politics of Thomas Jefferson: A Revisionist View.* (Lawrence, Kansas: University Press of Kansas, 1984), p. 70.

pg. 92: Meacham, Jon. *Thomas Jefferson: The Art of Power* (New York: Random House, 2013), p. 378.

pg. 94: *Ibid.*, p. 72.

pg. 94: *Ibid.* p. 73.

CHAPTER 6

pg. 99: Melton, Buckner F. Jr. *The Quotable Founding Fathers: A Treasury of 2,500 Wise and Witty Quotations From the Men and Women Who Created America* (Dulles, Virginia: Potomac Books, 2004), p. 145.

pg. 99: Adams, John. "Letter from John Adams to Abigail Adams, 19 December 1793," http://www.masshist.org/digitaladams/archive/doc?id=L17931219ja.

pg. 99: *Ibid.*

pg. 100: Meacham, Jon. *Thomas Jefferson: The Art of Power* (New York: Random House, 2013), p. 488.

pg. 100: *Ibid.*, p. 493.

pg. 100: *Ibid.*

pg. 103: Melton, Buckner F. Jr. *The Quotable Founding Fathers: A Treasury of 2,500 Wise and Witty Quotations From the Men and Women Who Created America* (Dulles, Virginia: Potomac Books, 2004), p. 55.

FURTHER INFORMATION

BOOKS

Beiswanger, William L., Peter J. Hatch, Lucia C. Stanton, and Susan R. Stein. *Thomas Jeffersons's Monticello*. Charlottesville, Virginia: The University of Virginia Press, 2002.

Ellis, Joseph J. American Sphinx: *The Character of Thomas Jefferson*. New York: Alfred A. Knopf, 1996.

Jefferson, Thomas. Ed. Merrill D. Peterson. *Thomas Jefferson: Writings*. New York: Literary Classics of the United States, 1984.

Meacham, Jon. Thomas Jefferson: *The Art of Power*. New York: Random House, 2013.

Wood, Gordon S. *Empire of Liberty: A History of the Early Republic, 1789–1815*. New York: Oxford University Press, 2009.

WEBSITES

The American Revolution
www.theamericanrevolution.org

This site features nearly everything a student would want to know about the Revolution, from its battles to the people who fought them to relevant documents. In addition to articles, it also features a timeline, videos, and online discussion boards.

Declaration of Independence

www.archives.gov/exhibits/charters/declaration.html

Explore the Declaration of Independence from the comfort of your home. The National Archive's webpage for the Declaration includes a brief history of the document, a text transcription, and a high-resolution scan of the original signed in Independence Hall, July 4, 1776.

Monticello

www.monticello.org

Jefferson's Monticello has been managed by the Thomas Jefferson Foundation since 1923. In addition to coordinating the estate's upkeep, the foundation also hosts Monticello.org, an invaluable resource for students of Jefferson. Here you will find articles on a broad range of topics, from a brief biography and a timeline of Jefferson's life to articles about Jefferson's major accomplishments and the daily life at Monticello during its prime.

Thomas Jefferson at the Library of Congress

www.loc.gov/exhibits/jefferson/

Thomas Jefferson created the seed of what would become the Library of Congress when he sold his library to the federal government. Today, the Library of Congress hosts a website about Jefferson. Sections include Monticello, the Virginia Republic, Jefferson and the American West, and, of course, Jefferson's library.

Thomas Jefferson at the Miller Center

millercenter.org/president/jefferson

The Miller Center at the University of Virginia hosts a detailed website on America's third president. In addition to links to longer articles on such topics as foreign and domestic policies during Jefferson's presidency, the Miller Center's site on Jefferson features facts at a glance, information about his cabinet members, and a photo gallery.

MUSEUMS AND ORGANIZATIONS

Independence Hall
nps.gov/inde

520 Chestnut St
Philadelphia, PA 19106

Library of Congress
loc.gov

101 Independence Ave SE
Washington, DC 20540

Monticello
monticello.org

931 Thomas Jefferson Pkwy
Charlottesville, VA 22902

National Archives
archives.gov

700 Pennsylvania Ave NW
Washington, DC 20408

BIBLIOGRAPHY

Daggett, Stephen. "Costs of Major U.S. Wars." Congressional Research Service. www.fas.org/sgp/crs/natsec/RS22926.pdf (accessed December 9, 2015).

"The Declaration of Independence." The Charters of Freedom. United States National Archives. Accessed December 9, 2015, http://www.archives.gov/exhibits/charters/declaration.html.

Ellis, Joseph J. *American Sphinx: The Character of Thomas Jefferson.* New York: Alfred A. Knopf, 1996.

"Embargo of 1807." Monticello.org. Accessed December 9, 2015, www.monticello.org/site/research-and-collections/embargo-1807.

"The Intolerable Acts." USHistory.org. Accessed December 9, 2015, www.ushistory.org/us/9g.asp.

Jefferson, Thomas. Ed. Kees de Mooy. *The Wisdom of Thomas Jefferson.* New York: Citadel Press Books, 2003.

Jefferson, Thomas. "Thomas Jefferson to Dabney Carr, 19 January 1816." Founders Online. Accessed December 9, 2015, founders. archives.gov/documents/Jefferson/03-09-02-0238.

Kukla, John. *A Wilderness So Immense: The Louisiana Purchase and the Destiny of America.* New York: Alfred A. Knopf, 2003.

Matthews, Richard K. *The Radical Politics of Thomas Jefferson: A Revisionist View*. Lawrence, Kansas: University Press of Kansas, 1984.

McCullough, David. *1776*. New York: Simon & Schuster, 2006.

Meacham, Jon. *Thomas Jefferson: The Art of Power*. New York: Random House, 2013.

Melton, Buckner F. Jr. *The Quotable Founding Fathers: A Treasury of 2,500 Wise and Witty Quotations From the Men and Women Who Created America*. Dulles, Virginia: Potomac Books, 2004.

Nash, Gary B. *The Unknown American Revolution: The Unruly Birth of Democracy and the Struggle to Create America*. New York: Penguin Group, 2005.

"Shays' Rebellion." US History.org. Accessed December 9, 2015, www.ushistory.org/us/15a.asp.

"Thomas Jefferson: A Brief Biography." Monticello.org. Accessed December 9, 2015, www.monticello.org/site/jefferson/thomas-jefferson-brief-biography.

"Thomas Jefferson and Sally Hemings: A Brief Account." Monticello.org. Accessed December 9, 2015, www.monticello.org/site/plantation-and-slavery/thomas-jefferson-and-sally-hemings-brief-account.

"Thomas Jefferson and the Virginia Statute for Religious Freedom." Virginia Historical Society. Accessed December 9, 2015, www.vahistorical.org/collections-and-resources/virginia-history-explorer/Thomas-Jefferson.

"Timeline of Jefferson's Life." Monticello.org. Accessed December 9, 2015, www.monticello.org/site/jefferson/timeline-jeffersons-life.

Tucker, Robert W. and David C. Hendrickson. *Empire of Liberty: The Statecraft of Thomas Jefferson*. New York: Oxford University Press, 1990.

Wood, Gordon S. *Empire of Liberty: A History of the Early Republic, 1789–1815*. New York: Oxford University Press, 2009.

———. *The Radicalism of the American Revolution: How a Revolution Transformed a Monarchical Society into a Democratic One Unlike Any That Had Ever Existed*. New York: Alfred A. Knopf, 1991.

Young, Ralph F. *Dissent in America: 400 Years of Speeches, Sermons, Arguments, Articles, Letters, and Songs That Made a Difference*. New York: Pearson Education, Inc., 2008.

INDEX

Page numbers in **boldface** are illustrations. Entries in **boldface** are glossary terms.

federal government, 68, 70, 72, 76–77, 80, 99
Federalists, 68, 70, 72–77
Franklin, Benjamin, 6, **43**, 50, 54, 58, 67, 96

Great Britain (*also* Britain *or* England), 6–7, 9, 21, 25–29, 31, 34, 36, 38, 44–45, 48, 50–51, 53, 57, 59, 64–65, 72, 75, 80–81, 85–86
gridlock, 97

Hemings, Sally, 90–91
Henry, Patrick, 38, 44, 48
House of Burgesses, Virginia, 10, 18, 23, 37–39, 44

Intolerable Acts/Coercive Acts, 36–37, 43–44, 60

Jefferson, Jane Randolph, 10, 13–15
Jefferson, Martha "Patty", 21, 90

Hamilton, Alexander, 68–74, 76–77
humanism, 21

Lee, Richard Henry, 44, 51
legislature, 18, 39, 67, 72, 75, 95
Lexington and Concord, 39–41, 43–45, 53
liberal, 22
Louisiana Purchase, 77, 80
loyalist, 29, 31, 36, 44, 51, 59

martial law, 35, 50, 53
migraine, 20
Monticello, 15–16, **15**, 67, 75, 84, 95, 98
mud slinging, 75

Napoleonic Wars, 80
neoclassical, 16

Parliament, 25–26, 28–30, 32, 34–35, 38–39, 80
partisanship, 75
patriots, 27, 32–34, 40, 61
philosophy, 9, 12, 19, 21–22, 45, 55, 83, 93, 99
plantation, 13, 16, 64, 84, 86, 93
press, 80
primogeniture, 64–65
Puritans, 29, 66
purview, 77

ABOUT THE AUTHOR

Andrew Coddington has a degree in creative writing from Canisius College. He has written several books for Cavendish Square, including *Henry David Thoreau: Writer of the Transcendentalist Movement* in the Great American Thinkers series. He lives in Lancaster, New York, with his fiancée and dog.